The World of THE NURSERY

GLADYS PETO

The World of THE NURSERY

Colin White

The Herbert Press

First published in Great Britain 1984 by
The Herbert Press Limited, 46 Northchurch Road, London N1 4EJ

Designed by Pauline Harrison
Edited by Penelope Miller

Typeset in Great Britain by Butler & Tanner Limited
Printed and bound in Hong Kong by South China Printing Co.

British Library Cataloguing in Publication Data

White, Colin
The world of the nursery.
1. Nurseries – Great Britain – Equipment and supplies – History 2. Children's furniture – Great Britain – History.
I. Title
645′.6 HQ784

ISBN 0 906969 34 4

Contents

The World of the Nursery
is dedicated to my wife Drusilla as a small
expression of my gratitude for the countless acts of
selflessness and devotion that have helped
to make the book possible.

Introduction

People who can see the world through the eyes of a child and can analyse it with the mind of an adult are few and privileged. Those who have the added ability to give artistic expression to such a vision are even more fortunate. *The World of the Nursery* is a record of some of the successes and failures that have taken place in the attempt to create those forms. It is a survey of items of artistic interest that might have been found in nurseries over a period of rather more than one hundred years; roughly the century from 1850 to 1950. It is an investigation into the artistic qualities of such things as cots, cribs and cradles, the patterns on curtains and rugs, the pictures hanging on nursery walls and the wall-coverings themselves. It looks at the illustrations in the books read to children, or from which they were later able to read for themselves. It examines decorative tiles and china, scrap-screens and silver: any nursery object, in fact, that shows evidence of somebody having cared about the way it looks. It is not exclusively a search for great art within the nursery, for there is much to be learnt from bad art as well as good, from lesser art as well as that which purports to be grand. Nursery art is no less significant when it is seen in the embroidery of a cot-cover rather than hanging framed on a wall.

Not all nursery art is art for the nursery. Burne Jones painted tile panels using the nursery themes of the Sleeping Beauty and Beauty and the Beast specifically as wall decorations for the dining-rooms of friends. The illustrator 'Alastair', one of the followers of Aubrey Beardsley, drew a fearsome 'Puss in Boots' solely as an essay in the grotesque. The surrealist illustrations of Salvador Dali's *Alice in Wonderland* are esoteric fantasies that no child could be expected to interpret. No matter how conducive to speculation such images may be, this book treats them as by-ways to the main theme.

It also avoids consideration of art done by children themselves. From samplers to paintings which rival in the power of their statements those of the Expressionists, children have depicted the world with a unique vision. It is a vision that has remained undisturbed by the arbitrary conventions made with pontifical solemnity by grown-ups whose opinions have repeatedly and shamelessly changed with fashion, offering subjective distortions that pretended to reveal to the child the true way of seeing.

This aspect of nursery art, fascinating though it is, already has an extensive literature of its own. For the same reason most toys, games, dolls and costume have been excluded. Sometimes, though, there are difficulties. Handkerchiefs manufactured in Britain depicting Mabel Lucie Attwell's 'Kiddiwinks', or their equivalent in the United States decorated with Palmer Cox's 'Brownies', relate to their respective book illustrations. If handkerchiefs are admissible, then why not pinafores or dresses using the same motifs? The Teddy Bear and the Pooh toys are essential in a book such as this; yet what of the many and equally engaging toys from less celebrated sources? The boundaries are ill-defined and are not always easy to determine.

Prams, which would not have been seen in the child's room itself, are an inherent part of the nursery world and have received mention in the book. And yet, even here, some items remain unclassifiable. A baby carriage that has at the front a movable horse deserves mention. What

1 The Queen's Dolls' House, exterior, 1924. Reproduced by Gracious Permission of Her Majesty the Queen.

2 The Queen's Dolls' House, day nursery, decorated by Edmund Dulac, 1924. Reproduced by Gracious Permission of Her Majesty the Queen.

then of the rocking-horse? Although it is now looked upon as a nursery toy and, as such, has been virtually excluded from this book, the rocking-horse was more than an elaboration of the hobby-horse: it was a functional object in the nursery and was intended to give the child the feel and motion of his future mode of transport and to teach him how to have a good 'seat'. The enchanting rocking-horse that Jessie M. King designed in 1916 cannot, for purely aesthetic reasons, be omitted. Has one, then, any justification for excluding the far more common Géricault-like 'neddies' that have graced so many nurseries?

In the same way, the magnificent Queen Mary's Dolls' House (1) at Windsor Castle was conceived by its architect Sir Edwin Lutyens, not as a house for dolls, but as a scaled-down version of a proper home, albeit for a princess. Everything in it, from the Rackham watercolour of 'Little Miss Muffett' to the tiny nursery chair, was specially created with this in mind. The designs and decorations reflected the thinking of artists and craftsmen of the 1920s. Any one of them might have been commissioned to submit designs such as these in full scale for a real house. Edmund Dulac's paintings of fairy tales on the walls of the day nursery (2) are as valid examples of art for the nursery as a Kate Greenaway wallpaper. Like the Noah's Ark mural that Carrie Stettheimer designed for the unique 'twenties dolls' house that is now in the Museum of the City of New York, the contents of these houses are often not toys but designs for Lilliputians.

In the end, as so often happens, the choice of what is to be included and what omitted has been a personal one. The taste and whim of the author have been the determinants, and nowhere has this licence to select been more indulged than in the case of the illustrated nursery books.

Of all aspects of the nursery, picture books have been found in all nurseries at all times. More than any other object in the nursery they have recorded the changes in fashion and outlook of the adult's, and hence the child's, world. Illustration has never been one of the innovative forces in the world of fine art, but nevertheless the nursery book is the armature around which any survey of nursery art has to be constructed. The whole story of art for the nursery may be found in the pictures in the children's books of the last century.

Although *The World of the Nursery* gives precedence to the British nursery, the United States of America and, to a lesser extent, Australia, are referred to throughout the book. Together, these three regions give some insight into the different stages of development of the nursery and its art. The British nursery has been a product of a society that developed by refinement and differentiation. At its peak, towards the end of the nineteenth century, it reflected the layers of exclusivity that maintained artificial class-groupings outside the family and the very real age-groupings within.

The rise of the nursery, in a society which rationalized its motives by combining a paternalism with a desire for the privacy that was a natural consequence of increased possessions, was as inevitable as its decline in the present age of egalitarianism and changed attitudes towards parental care. Today the nursery, if not atrophying as an anachronism, is, at the least, in a state of metamorphosis. Conveniently, all this has taken place over a period of little more than one hundred years.

The research for this book has provided many joys of discovery. The existence of Joe Painter's vast collection of chamber-pots in Norfolk; Jack Hampshire's Baby Carriage Museum in Kent, with its more than three hundred examples of the art of the pram; and the wonderful dolls' house in New York, with its figures of Gertrude Stein, Marcel Duchamp and Virgil Thomson, were all notable 'finds'.

In helping me to discover these and other delights many people have been unbelievably generous with their time and knowledge. Some have become friends, others have remained anonymous as workers in libraries and other institutions who have been given the task of looking up some particular fact that I needed. The omission of their names, as of any others whom, by oversight, I have not mentioned, in no way lessens my gratitude and indebtedness to them for all their help and interest.

I wish to thank in particular the following individuals for the special way in which each one has helped in the making of this book: C. Richard Aldin-Becker, Felicity Ashbee, David Cuppleditch, Ann Hysa Dorfsman, Dorothy Duncan, Kathy Elgin, Pauline Flick, Karen Fowler, Doris Frohnsdorff, Deena Gavins, Janet Goose, Stuart and Margaret Green, Marian Hahn, Jean Hamilton, Jack Hampshire, Robin Hartley, Joan Hassall, John Hayes, Tony Herbert, Ann Hughey, Diana Johnson, C. Peter Kaellgren, Hans van Lemmen, T.F. Lane, Ellen Langlands, Fiona MacCarthy, Dr E. Wolfgang Mick, Pixie O'Harris, George H. Pipal,

Lawrence V. Seeborg, Maisy Stapleton, Merle Taylor, Tasha Tudor, Clive Wainwright, Deborah White, Jeremy White, John Wilks.

In addition, the following people, companies and institutions have been kind enough to allow me to reproduce photographs of material for which they hold the copyright:

Angus & Robertson Publishers, (c22), (115), (133), (138); Blackie Publishing Group Ltd., Scotland, (c21), (189); Bradford Art Galleries & Museums, (c2), (12), (24), (42), (78), (79); Curtis Brown Ltd., London, (c33), (137), (163); Campbell's Soups Inc., (159); Canadian Pacific Corporate Archives Collection, (77); Constable and Co., (93); Tom Cooke, (199); Cooper-Hewitt Museum, The Smithsonian Institution's National Museum of Design, (c11), (c37), (65), (70), (72), (76); Coward McCann & Geoghegan Inc., (168); Serge Danot, (197); Crown Decorative Products Ltd., (186); The Edison Institute (Henry Ford Museum and Greenwich Village), (19); Barbara Edwards, (99), (136); Pauline Flick, (c8), (43), (58), (59); Gladstone Pottery Museum, Stoke-on-Trent, (c24), (125), (127); Grosvenor Museum, Chester, (c3), (25), (32); Jack Hampshire, The Baby Carriage Museum, Kent, (106), (107), (108), (109); Hancock Shaker Village Inc., Massachussetts, (9); Heal & Sons Ltd., (190), (192), (193), (194), (195), (196); A.E. Hoad & Co., (c22); Hodder & Stoughton Ltd., (198); Ironbridge Gorge Museum Trust, (123); Piers Kurrein, (188); Lucie Attwell Ltd., (c10), (28), (75), (94), (158); Lund Humphreys Publishers, (8); Margowen Inc., New York, (187); Lady Martin, (112), (113); The Medici Society Ltd., (c20), (83), (84); Museum of Childhood, Edinburgh, (c4), (c6), (c9), (c10), (27), (28), (29), (32), (152), (160); Museum of Costume & Textiles, Nottingham, (117); Museum of the City of New York, (7), (16), (17), (23); Thomas Nelson & Sons U.K. Ltd., (c35); Oxford University Press, (169); The Estate of W.H. Robinson, (93), (145); The Preservation Society of Newport County, Rhode Island, (c1), (22); Puffin Books, (145); The Putnam Publishing Group, (168); Paul Rand, (200); Random House Inc., (88), (171); The Executors of the late Miss E.M. Robinson, (39), (148); Royal Doulton Tableware Ltd., (50), (51), (52), (53), (131), (132); Arthur Sanderson & Sons Ltd., (c38); Charles Scribner's Sons Inc., (137); The Spastic Centre of N.S.W. and the N.S.W. Society of Crippled Children, (114); Stoke-on-Trent Museum & Art Gallery, (63); © United Feature Syndicate Inc., (c40), (201); Victoria & Albert Museum, (10), (15), (18), (21), (26), (47), (66), (69), (181), (182); Viking Penguin Inc., New York, (170); © Walt Disney Enterprises Ltd., (188); Frederick Warne P.L.C., (129), (130); Josiah Wedgwood & Sons Ltd., (56), (62), (64); Wenham Historical Association & Museum Inc., (c5); Whitworth Art Gallery, University of Manchester, (c13), (67); William Morris Gallery, (118), (126); Matvyn Wright, (198).

Numbers in brackets refer to the monochrome illustrations. Numbers preceded by c refer to the colour plates.

The chapter heading decorations are by Charles Robinson, courtesy of the Executors of the late Miss E.M. Robinson.

Primary sources of the reproduced book illustrations are noted in the captions, together with special acknowledgments. Other copyright holders are listed here. The author has made every effort to clear all rights. He would be glad to hear from any copyright claimant he has inadvertently failed to contact.

CHAPTER I

The Growth of the Nursery

Nurseries are not usually found in log cabins. Nor are they found in crofts or the back-to-back houses of industrial towns in the North of England. Nomads and pioneers do not have nurseries. Nor do the poor. A nursery is a 'room of one's own' and this, by implication, means that there must be other rooms in the house, and hence a certain level of stability, both economic and in permanence of tenure. Nurseries and schoolrooms were not uncommon in the eighteenth century, but the nursery as we know it was essentially a product of the Victorian age: certain, inalterable and God-fearing.

In the early part of the nineteenth century the Industrial Revolution helped to create a new group of largely self-made men who, with newly found riches, wished to associate with their peers in wealth and to penetrate the society of the upper classes which, previously, had been denied them. The desire for emulation was not merely a form of flattery; it was an attempt to assume some of the aura and magic of the chosen model. By aping the great, some of the mystique of that greatness could be transferred and, like the King's Touch, transform the supplicant.

There were two ways of entering that society. One was by offering wealth as an inducement for intermarriage with the scions of the upper classes. The other was to create an environment in which the society – the one which dictated manners, taste and fashion – could feel at ease or, even better, in awe. To own a town house was good. To build a country house of splendour was ideal. Between approximately 1830 and 1870 many of the vast country houses, whose names are now part of the Sunday round of open-day visiting, were built. Superb homes were commissioned from the great architects of the day by engineering manufacturers and mill owners who sought to relate their manner of living to the success of their financial speculations. The most influential of these architects was Alfred Pugin whose advocacy of the Gothic style, as the one most fitting to express the worthiness of British architecture, was eagerly accepted by his reverential clients.

Pugin was an architect who believed in the sanctity of individual privacy. He was a 'room man' who maintained that specific areas of the house should have specialized functions. It was he who, in his first-floor plans, conceived of distinct night and day nurseries, with the nurse's bedroom, bathroom and scullery as a suite linked by the nursery corridor to the master bedroom. Once the living area of the child was demarcated the way became clear for the advent of the nanny. Babies can indeed be fractious, children a nuisance and grown-ups selfish of their time. What began as a help for the mother developed by degrees into a convenient way of transferring responsibility. Fortunately, not all such delegation proved destructive. George Bernard Shaw, brought up in Dublin by a nanny, declared that his mother's almost total neglect of him led to a relationship in which there were no sordid or disillusioning contacts and that, as a result, he idolized her. The mother could remain the untarnished ideal. The nanny was the practical reality, bringing order and discipline, as well as comfort and solace, to the nursery.

The example had been made and the message received. The lesser captains of industry adopted the pattern according to their means and the space available. Children were to be nurslings at home until fledged. If they were to be looked upon as dependents, and not as imperfect adults sprung ready from the womb, facilities had to be provided to encourage the careful rearing of the children but, at the same time, to permit as little interference as possible with the everyday life of the parents. There was more than a half-truth in the thought that the nursery was initially a device for filtering the aggression of the infant and producing a tranquil child to be inspected and approved by its parents at the end of the day.

The nursery could only exist where affluence and social convention allowed the child to be set apart, either as an individual with special needs that could only be dealt with in discreet surroundings, or as an intruder into the more structured life of the parent. For this there was needed an unlimited supply of cheap labour and, conveniently, in an age of limited educational opportunity and restricted transport (the two outlets that might have helped people to better their position) there was an ample supply of living-in domestic help. In Victorian England it was not difficult to find suitable candidates whose duties as housemaids could be expanded to those of nursemaids and ultimately nannies. Families were large: an outcome of religious bias against, and ignorance of, what were in any case minimal methods of contraception. In addition, a larger number of children offered a greater certainty of survival of the family name in an age of untrammelled disease. Where circumstances permitted, large families, large houses and cheap labour meant that the physical running of the home could be entrusted to a servant body which itself needed living quarters, and so a division of the house came into being: the 'below stairs' and the 'above'. Within this grading of the household, with the nursery in a position accessible to the mother, the nurse acted as the lieutenant of the mother, and both child and nurse were allocated a room in the upper part of the house. Here the child could be tended and the parents have freedom of access whilst being spared the noise of daily combat or, as the German writer Herman Muthesius suggested in his book *The English House* which dealt with the British way of life at the beginning of the twentieth century: 'The nursery is a place where the children can enjoy a full measure of peace without their lives being disturbed by the activities of the grown-ups.'

Traditionally nannies were 'Nurses', as in the case of Juliet's confidante. The person called 'Nanny' was a later recasting of the elderly person to whom the child addressed its version of the word 'Grandma'. The aspiring nanny often joined a household at the age of twelve or thirteen already having experience of caring for a number of her own siblings. She would start as a nursery maid and, along with one or two others, would be responsible for the upkeep of the nursery quarters under the supervision of the existing nanny. With age she would have been given greater responsibility with the children themselves until death, dismissal or retirement resulted in another series of upgradings within the household.

The nanny ruled supreme in the nursery. As a specialist her opinion was deferred to. The children were her children, and only on temporary loan to the mother. They were brought up speaking in nanny's accent and with her grammar until the time came for a governess, so very often a 'distressed gentlelady', to put things right. The children were subject to the nanny's fundamentalist God-fearing nature, fortified by folk lore and folk remedies, from laxatives to leeches. Above all, the nanny, in common with so many of the 'upper' servants, tended to develop snobbish airs that could put restraint on the child and inhibit its own self-levelling tendencies. The nanny was the moving object that the newly hatched chick walks after under the impression that this is the mother. As such, she was in the unassailable position of forming or, as often happened, deforming the character of a child during its most receptive years.

For a long time, children had been treated as smaller versions of adults in their dress, food and drink. Down the ages, portraits of the children of the nobility had shown them, in costume and deportment, as proto-adults. With boys as well as girls dressed in skirts until the age of six, being 'breeched' was as ceremonial an event as being confirmed, and adult manners and behaviour were expected of them as early as possible (3).

3 Nursery plate: 'Just Breeched', maker unknown, *c.* 1850. Private collection.

This attitude, although in the main long abandoned, has persisted to the present day in the ceremonial of presenting the child with a christening set. These are tokens of responsibility from the godparent to the adult that it is hoped the child will become. Christening cups, the very form of which points to a use as an ale-bearing rather than a milk-bearing vessel, are not meant for children. Consequently, their decoration has posed its own problems. An English silver-gilt christening cup from the middle of the nineteenth century (4) was designed and decorated true to its material and its purpose as a drinking cup. Its design of acanthus leaves harmonized well with the rococo handle and the gentle swell of the cover. The decoration of a slightly later cup made by J. C. Edington reflected, in its complex chasework, the heavy Gothic romanticism of its time. The design, in heavy relief, of a cavalier surrounded by symbols of the chase might well have been intended to illustrate the nursery rhyme 'Bye Baby Bunting, Daddy's gone a-hunting' (5), but more probably related to the interests and life-style of the donor and the parent. The classical maidens on the accompanying knife, fork and spoon (6), especially the one gracing the beautifully designed blade of the knife, could possibly be looked upon as

C1 Child's desk, *c.* 1880. Kingscote, Newport, Rhode Island.

4 (right) Christening cup, silver-gilt, *c.* 1850; height 4¼ in. Leeds City Art Galleries (Lotherton Hall).

5 (far right) Christening cup, silver, by J. Chas. Edington, 1856; height 4 in. Leeds City Art Galleries (Lotherton Hall).

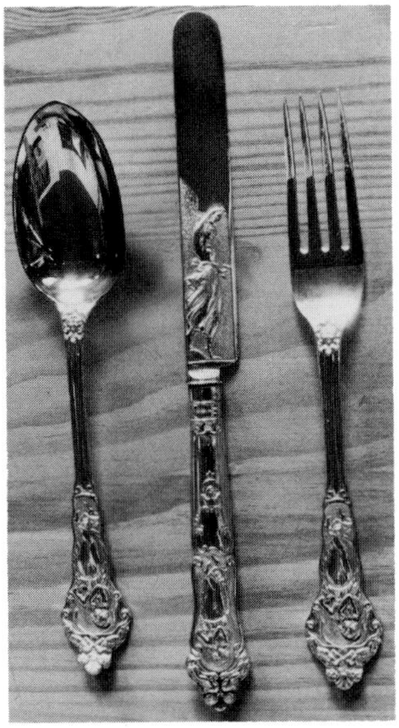

6 (above) Christening cutlery set, silver, by George Adams, 1855; knife 8¾ in., fork 7¼ in., spoon 7¼ in. Leeds City Art Galleries (Lotherton Hall).

7 (above right) Christening set, bowl and plate, silver, by Tiffany & Co., 1893. Museum of the City of New York; gift of Miss Isabel Shults.

angels and therefore more suited to the child. The dilemma arose from the fact that to introduce nursery themes into the medium of engraved or chased silver was to allow the romping world of the child to conflict with something that was essentially serious, dignified and sober.

Tiffany's in New York manufactured christening sets of exquisite workmanship with scenes from fairy stories and nursery rhymes, or friezes of child soldiers, which attempted to circumvent the fundamental purpose of the christening set by trying to placate the child (7). Their splendour was undeniable but their theme attempted the impossible task of combining frivolity with ceremonial formality. Far more appropriate was the christening mug that C.R. Ashbee, that great teacher of Arts and Crafts principles, designed for his own daughter in 1913 (8). One would be hard put to find a more beautiful expression of fitness for purpose than this simple and graceful object.

The ceremony and regalia associated with christening were bound up, in mid-Victorian times, with the worrying fear of Original Sin. The child was considered a potential monster: a porous vessel readily permeated by Satan. It was strongly held that only through religion, education and chastisement, both physical and mental, could his salvation be achieved. The staff with which to retrieve the stray lamb became the rod with which to exorcise the Devil. Childhood was an apprenticeship in which adult precepts were to be taught in an adult fashion, with images of an adult nature used to guide the child into an adult world. Frivolity was, at the least, mere time-wasting and, at the worst, the work of Satan. In an age when illness was ever present and child mortality high, indolence was playing the Devil's game. The hardness of life on earth was the entrance fee for the rewards of Heaven. The eighteenth and nineteenth centuries in Britain assaulted the child's mind in the same way, and for the same purpose, that the parents of Sparta were supposed to have tormented the child's body. Those children who survived the initiation were fit to join the community. The fact that the child was a special person with his own, albeit egocentric, viewpoint and needs was not generally accepted until the second half of the nineteenth century.

It might be supposed that in the United States and Australia, both of them pioneering countries, nurseries and the accompanying code of ethics would have developed at a parallel stage, when wealth, and the desire to shield it from outside intrusion, came to a successful few. In fact, when the very earliest homes came to be built for the wealthier settlers the inclusion of a nursery was not even considered. The daily life of the children was shared with that of the parents, and no distinction was made between the order of their existence and that of the rest of the family. People who had emigrated to these countries had done so to carve an existence out of a new land. Every working unit of the family was expected to contribute to the family welfare according to its capacity for labour. A separate nursery would have required either servant help or the usurping of the offices of an able-bodied older child.

In America all members of the community, however unequal they might have been with regard to basic wealth, felt themselves equal with regard to individual dignity. Consequently, servant labour, other than slave labour, was not easy to find. People who were incapable of improving their existence in a land of such opportunity were considered to be equally incapable of becoming responsible servants. In some of the communal religious groups that had grown up in New England especially, the welfare of the children was approached in an advanced and enlightened manner that was not to be achieved in more 'sophisticated' societies for a considerable time. It was a significant part of this ethic that child-rearing was an 'enfolding' and not, as was so common in that age, a delegating of responsibility. The care and concern that was part of the daily life of these

C2 Nursery at the Mill Owner's House, Bradford Industrial Museum, Yorkshire.

8 Christening cup, silver, by C.R. Ashbee, 1912; height 3¾ in. Collection of Felicity Ashbee.

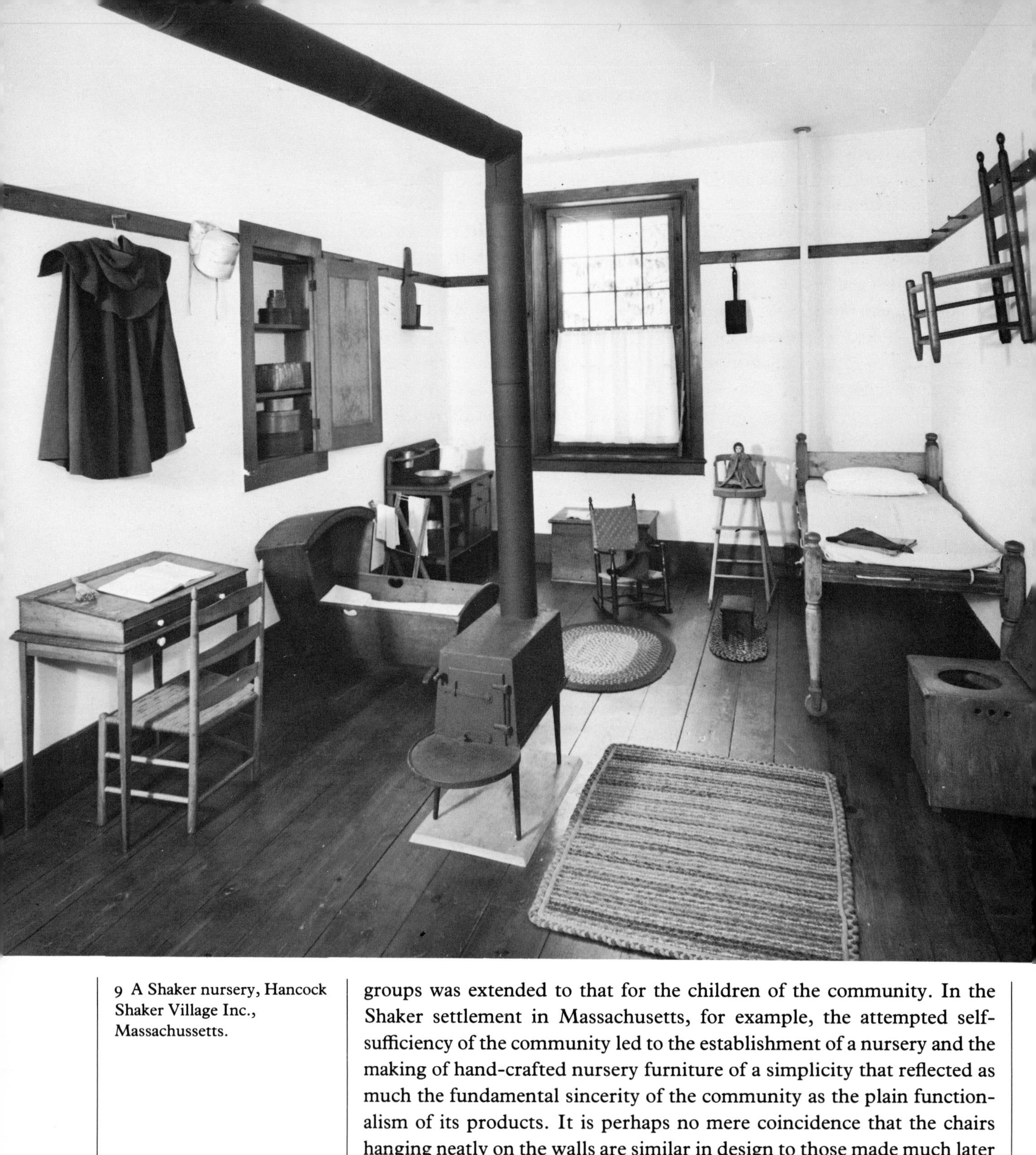

9 A Shaker nursery, Hancock Shaker Village Inc., Massachussetts.

groups was extended to that for the children of the community. In the Shaker settlement in Massachusetts, for example, the attempted self-sufficiency of the community led to the establishment of a nursery and the making of hand-crafted nursery furniture of a simplicity that reflected as much the fundamental sincerity of the community as the plain functionalism of its products. It is perhaps no mere coincidence that the chairs hanging neatly on the walls are similar in design to those made much later in the workshops of William Morris by men who shared the same desire to be truthful to the materials used (9), (10).

In Australia, when the country was first being developed, there was a relatively large working-class population from which many of the womenfolk sought work in domestic service. Yet, because of the comparatively lesser opulence of the community in general, it was not until the beginning of the twentieth century that the nursery became a recognized feature of the larger Australian houses. Only then, with success and increased leisure time did there develop a more liberal attitude towards child rearing that began in Europe and spread outwards. The obsession with the religious purification of the new-born sinner was gradually replaced everywhere by an ever-increasing genuflection towards the new-born angel. Although this attitude happened early in the history of the nursery in Australia it took longer to develop in the more established world of the British nursery. The layer of middle-class people who, through outstanding ability or good fortune, had risen above the poverty of their surroundings needed a code of conduct for survival: a rationalization of their aloofness and a nucleus around which to coalesce. This nucleus, as with all hermetic orders, was Discipline: the one feature that the undifferentiated masses were felt to lack. Whatever undermined that discipline was held to weaken the foundations of Society. Hence the obsessive drive to improve the mind and soul, and the desire to find fulfilment in the achievement of the children. The importance of the child was based not on the uniqueness of his personality but on his role as a budding contributor to the orderliness and preservation of the system. The nursery was the training ground and the parade ground. Once the concept of nursery upbringing became an accepted fact, the way was open for the flood of decorative and ornamental devices that came to constitute 'art for the nursery'.

10 Nursery chair, painted and ebonized wood, William Morris, *c.* 1879. Victoria & Albert Museum.

CHAPTER 2

Nursery Furnishings

The early nursery was the nurse's room in all but name. It was decorated cheaply, as were all servants' rooms, with furniture transferred from the rest of the house. Tables and chairs for the children were often no more than adult furniture sawn down to size but, although the legs were shortened for use by little children, the scale of the chairs and tables often betrayed their adult origin in their squatness and incongruity, with seats too long for little legs and sides too far away to support little arms. It was only in those items of furniture that had to be devised especially for the newly born that the individuality of the nursery could be expressed.

An infant's first 'bed', a generic term, was a 'cradle'; sometimes no more than a simple wooden box with rockers extending outwards from the sides for a nurse's foot to provide the rocking. More elaborate was the 'bassinet': a hooded cradle of wickerwork or basketwork, and so called because of its basin-like shape although, for a short time during the nineteenth century, it was referred to as a 'berceaunette' (11), it being felt that French cradles were of a better lineage than English basins. A 'crib' was a small rectangular bed with barred or latticed sides and without any rocking facilities. A 'cot' was a child's bed suspended to swing between two uprights (12). What nowadays the British refer to as a 'cot' or 'folding cot' is really a crib with locking sides which can drop down at the touch of a latch for ease of access.

11 The 'Berceaunette', 1872.

Where the mother or, as frequently happened, the grandmother, was allowed to indulge her fancy, from layette to bassinet an inflorescence of lawn, silks and laces, pleated, frilled and ruched, provided the baby with warmth, comfort and a suitable stage-setting. The bassinet was raised

12 Cot, wood and cane, *c.* 1870. Bradford Industrial Museum.

13 Baby bath, papier maché, Jennens & Bettridge, London, 1851.

from the floor for convenience in bending down, and its lined curtains offered protection from draughts. The work-basket containing the layette would be a similar hand-made confection of delicate fabrics, and even the baby's bath could come in forms like the luxurious composition of papier maché that was shown at the Great Exhibition of 1851 (13). Those attending the exhibition could also order from Mr Winfield's of Birmingham a child's cot of uncommon workmanship (14). This, carved and scrolled in rococo splendour, was a shell in which the baby could lie, like a cygnet of Neuschwanstein, under the soothing gaze of a cast metal Guardian Angel.

14 'Mr Winfield's cot', 1851.

15 Rocking cradle with clockwork mechanism, after Thomas Sheraton; height $37\frac{3}{4}$ in., length 36 in. Victoria & Albert Museum.

Some member of a large family would always, in the overlapping nature of generations, have children. Their cradles and cots, whether plain and sturdy, made with minimal decoration by local craftsmen, or manufactured commercially, like the magnificent cot of the 1870s with its ogee hood, would be passed round a family for many years (12). An even more sumptuous heirloom would have been the richly made cradle (15) taken from a design by Thomas Sheraton, which incorporated a clockwork movement that allowed the baby to be rocked non-stop, if so desired, for forty-eight hours. With nursery furniture, as with all crafted things, one paid for workmanship and quality of design. The rosewood crib (16) made in the Renaissance style by the French cabinet-maker Alexander Roux, who was working in New York in the 1850s at a time when the fashion for French inspired design was at its peak, is an example of the excellence that could be achieved in the manufacture of nursery furniture. The carved and fretted sides have a lightness, almost a frivolity, that contrasts well with the more sober head- and foot-boards with their caps of severe classical scrolls.

Only a wealthy family could afford nursery furniture as elaborate as this crib or the children's chair made by John Henry Belter, again in New

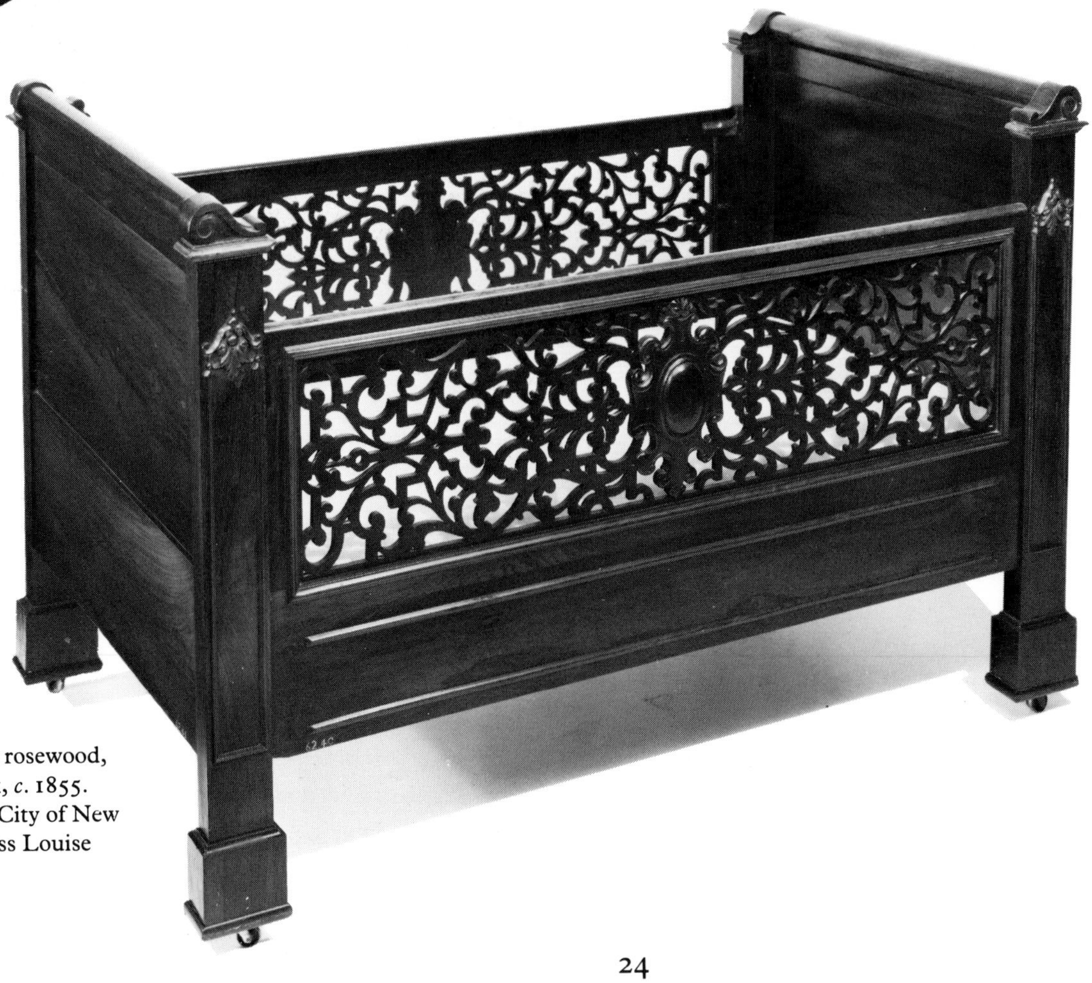

16 Child's crib, rosewood, Alexander Roux, *c.* 1855. Museum of the City of New York; gift of Miss Louise Coskery.

17 John Henry Belter: adult armchair and matching child's chair, laminated rosewood, *c.* 1856. Museum of the City of New York; gift of Mr and Mrs Gunther Vietor.

York in the 1850s, as a miniature version of an adult model (17). It was a chair for a little autocrat: a padded throne in red velvet and rosewood created for someone born to rule. One did not crawl into such a chair, one ascended. It was Belter who introduced into the United States the European invention of 'Bentwood' which, in its simplest form, was plywood. This permitted the construction of complicated shapes without the hazards and expense of hand-carving large pieces of wood. It was especially useful for the simpler curves needed in the construction of high-chairs. An ingenious but somewhat cumbersome specimen, made in England in the late nineteenth century, was convertible into a low-seated rocking-

18 Folding high chair, laminated wood, *c.* 1890. Victoria & Albert Museum.

chair, and the contrast between its turned and pedimented classical back and the complex function of the rest of the chair gave it a delightful incongruity (18).

Children's versions of adult furniture were common, and the ubiquitous Windsor chair was copied in miniature with great success. An early American double rocking-chair for adult and baby, with a special guard rail to prevent the child tipping out, was an interesting variation, especially in the example shown with its folk decoration reminiscent of the art of fairground or barge painting (19). Windsor high-chairs, however, were a failure, for their disproportionately long legs gave them a giraffe-like appearance (20). Good designs for high chairs have always been difficult to achieve, and solutions to the problem of combining function with pleasing design have rarely been successful even in modern times. Indeed, the interpretation of the term 'good design' has always been a point of controversy in the world of arts and crafts. The little nursery chair made by William Morris in 1879 followed his principle that good design was an outcome of function. With its rush seat and lightly turned rails serving to accentuate its form, the chair still appears thoroughly modern because of its very simplicity (10). By contrast, a unique cradle, made in 1865 by the architect and designer Norman Shaw, is a masterly example of the type of decorated furniture that was inspired by the Pre-Raphaelitism of its time (21). The hood, lined in dark green, with a pattern of the sun and stars in gold, was coffered on the outside and had in each panel a bird set against a gold background. The panels on the sides bore the signs of the Zodiac and, at the head, guarding the child, were carved dogs seated on posts.

19 Double Windsor rocking-chair, maple and pine, *c.* 1830. The Henry Ford Museum, Dearborn, Michigan.

20 (below left) Windsor high chair, *c.* 1900. Courtesy Phillips, Leeds.

21 (below right) The Norman Shaw crib, oak, with lifting head, 1867: height 42 in., length 42 in., width 20¼ in. Victoria & Albert Museum.

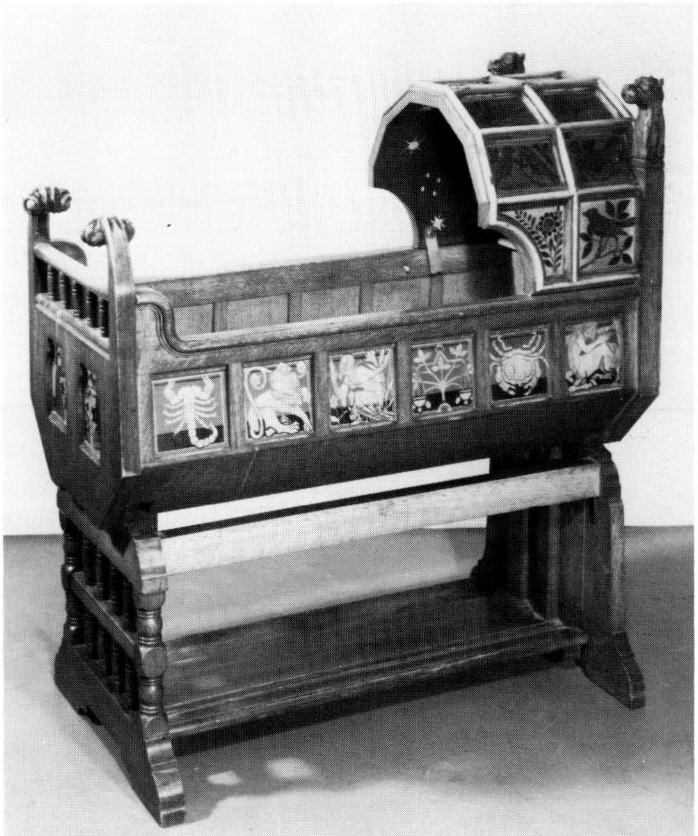

The cradle as a whole could be made to rock on its base by means of a treadle, giving an added fantasy to an object that already belonged more to medieval romance than to a Victorian nursery.

Whenever the parents could afford to indulge themselves the nursery tended to become less an outhouse than a showpiece, sometimes a shrine, within the home. Considerations of beauty and taste often outweighed practicality as a consideration. The exquisite mahogany desk (C1) made at the turn of the century for the nursery at Kingscote in Newport Rhode Island, hardly seems sturdy enough for everyday use by children.

22 Baby pillow, *c.* 1875. Chateau sur Mer, Newport, Rhode Island.

Similarly, the beautiful baby pillow (22) in the Wilmot home of Chateau-sur-Mer, another of the so-called Newport 'cottages', is decorated with intricate appliqué work that, although perfect for display, hardly offers the smoothest of surfaces for a baby's cheek. A photograph taken in 1896 of the nursery of the Donavan family of New Jersey shows a consistency about the decorations that could only have been brought about by a single guiding hand (23). The wallpaper, although it does not have a nursery theme, has a simple pattern which picks up that of the chintz used for covering the settee and the chairs, the mantelpiece, and the door curtains which served as draught excluders. It was a nursery which combined the purpose-built with the expedient. The carpet and the little occasional table are obvious appropriations from elsewhere. The mantelshelf ornaments, adult in taste, are meant, if not for the enhancement of the photograph, for the delectation of the nurse or visitors. All the other items in the room, whether for adult or child, seem to have been assembled expressly for the nursery.

23 The nursery at the Donavan residence, New Jersey, 1896. Photograph courtesy the Museum of the City of New York.

Totally different from the Donavan nursery was one dating from the same late-Victorian period in the home of a mill-owner in Bradford, Yorkshire (C2). The relative harshness of life in an industrial community in the North of England, the grime, the unrelenting rain and fog of the region, and the stringent sense of propriety in the Victorian home, were reflected in the heaviness, the solidity and the variegated nature of the furnishings which, like a portmanteau word sought to embrace all possibilities. Both the heating stove (24), safer than the open fireplace of the

Donavan nursery, and the washstand are decorated with a selection of tiles, in black and buff illustrating scenes from Sir Walter Scott, designed by J. Moyr Smith in 1875 for Minton's. The washstand itself, of simple natural pine, ribbed with constant scrubbing, is rendered elaborate only by the shape imposed on it by the mirrorwork and the abundance of its shelves and recesses. Its design is functional without any concession to superficial decoration or frivolity. The swinging cot, with its plaited cane sides and Gothic arched hood, is raised high on a stand; its light mesh allowing it to be moved easily and, at the same time, let the baby see and be seen. The papered walls are covered with pictures, both secular and religious and, in the corner of the room stands a scrap screen (C3), (25).

Draughts were always a problem in the home. The curtains covering the doors, the raising of a cot from the floor and the use of adequate screens were all attempts to exclude the uncomfortable and often dangerous streams of cold air that came from the use of combustible fuels for heating. Nursery screens were a convenient solution and were used not only as draught excluders but also as movable partitions for concealment and division of space. They were often decorated with that typical Victorian speciality the 'scrap'. Cutting, clipping and sticking things were occupational pastimes for children in the days when entertainment was still considered an activity. Embossed and highly coloured decorated paper shapes, printed mainly in Bavaria by chromolithography and intended originally for cake decoration, became part of the ornament of a page in every child's scrap album. As the collecting of scraps became a hobby in itself the number and types proliferated. Every aspect of fantasy and reality was depicted. Children, serious and with eyes dark-ringed and exophthalmic, posed with shrimp-nets or hoops; cats and dogs played football; clowns blew musical instruments; Chinamen, always dressed in Imperial robes, rivalled in splendour Scotsmen in full Highland dress, and Her Majesty or the Prince of Wales appeared frequently, as if to reassure the family that all was right with the world as long as the Empire flourished.

24 Nursery stove, with tiles designed by J. Moyr Smith for Minton, *c.* 1880. The Bradford Industrial Museum.

25 Scrap screen, *c.* 1890. Grosvenor Museum, Chester.

Scraps were gummed onto boxes and small pieces of furniture, and reached their apotheosis in the adornment of the large irresistible surfaces of the nursery screens. On these the elaborate iconography of the scraps released latent surrealist tendencies as illustrations, unrelated in time or scale, were stuck side by side. Their deliberate disarray echoed the scattered profusion of the contents of the nurseries themselves. The impression given; and the Bradford nursery was typical of many of its time, was one of extemporization, with little sense of anybody having taken the trouble to relate the contents to the dimensions of a child's world. The nursery was primarily an adult's room, and the manner of its furnishing acknowledged this. The child, as was true of its position within the family, was scarcely more than a decorative appendage.

CHAPTER 3

The Victorian Child

26 The Astley Cooper chair, *c.* 1865. Victoria & Albert Museum.

Love for the child was not lacking in the Victorian home; it was merely tempered by rules. 'To be seen and not heard' was the desired quality and, as with many precepts, what started as a rule of thumb came to be thought of as a rule of God, and a justification for adult selfishness and bigotry. It implied that the child was an intruder into the business of life and that he must be made to understand the limits of his territory. The structure of Victorian society, presented as a hierarchy of the Church, the Queen, Parliament, the Navy, Papa, Mama, Nanny and me, was held to be the foundation of Britain's greatness. Correct behaviour was what offered no divergence from and no threat to the existing order of things. Children, unfortunately, were an anarchic element who were not born ready instructed in that sense of order. They had to be moulded in both body and mind in the God-ordained pattern. The new-born infant was revered, but the growing child had to conform, and the inborn slovenliness, mental and physical, corrected. Posture was important. The notorious Astley Cooper chair, with its straight back and lack of foot rest, ensured that any departure from an upright position meant misery for the sitter (26).

Cleanliness was, of course, next to Godliness, but in a way more than the glib use of the phrase acknowledged, for it was that very ritual cleansing, of both body and spirit, that ensured the preservation of the Christian ethic. The fervour with which adult authority carried out this practice was beautifully preserved in 'You Dirty Boy', one of the advertisement figures for Pears' soap (27). Nobody in Victorian times thought of manufacturing soap in shapes attractive to children. Novelty soaps for the nursery did not appear until as late as 1910, but when they did, usually hand-painted with non-toxic paints, they were quickly taken up by manufacturers and became an accepted part of the nursery ceremonial (28), (29).

Thrift, too, was always encouraged in the nursery, and money boxes in metal and pottery as well as other durable but rarely raid-proof materials, played their part in the upbringing of every child. Money boxes, more than any other items in the nursery, stimulated designers to produce ingenious novelties in forms as varied as animals, fruit, letter boxes and all manner of household appliances (30). Some of the most attractive were the mechanical ones, made of cast iron and beautifully painted, that were

27 (left) 'You Dirty Boy', biscuitware of a Pears' soap figurine, *c.* 1900. Museum of Childhood, Edinburgh.

28 Mabel Lucie Attwell: nursery soap, *c.* 1930. Museum of Childhood, Edinburgh.

29 Novelty soap, *c.* 1920. Museum of Childhood, Edinburgh.

C3 Scrap screen (detail), *c.* 1890. Grosvenor Museum, Chester.

manufactured in the United States in the last quarter of the nineteenth century (C4), (31). By pressing a button an eagle could be made to feed its young with a coin, a mule could be made to kick a penny back into the open mouth of a startled farmhand, or a navvy be made to toss a coin from his hod up to a workmate on the storey above. Humorous money boxes were made with well-known characters from both British and American children's comics, ranging from Little Orphan Annie to Teddy Tail. Pottery money boxes could be found in designs as varied as the exotic Buckley ware, made from the mottled clays found around Chester (32); the ubiquitous ivy-clad thatched cottages, and the modern versions of the piggy bank in pastel colours and decorated in meretricious abandon with pretty flowers.

Failure to live up to the ethics of Godliness, Cleanliness and Thrift was Naughtiness and this, graded in severity from peccadillos to Sin, brought its appropriate punishments with the ultimate threat of Hell and Damnation for Evermore which, for a child, was longer than next week. Sin, like Ether, was believed to fill the Universe, and the child's progress through life was a constant struggle against this all-pervasive medium. In primers of objects to be found in the nursery of the 1850s, 'Rod' was as common and as unremarkable as 'Bath' (33). Corporal punishment, like a meat tenderizer, was expected to soften up the child and make him more receptive to improvement.

Goodness, however, brought rewards. Good deeds began with respect for grown-ups, kindness to animals, servants and slaves, in that order: the only divisions of a household known to a well-brought up child. Rewards ranged from 'the Treat' to the intangible and imperfectly understood heights of 'Eternal Bliss in Heaven'.

Work and application were considered holy in those days when God was wrathful and religion was a message of thunder, caveat and threat. The child, like the criminal, was generally looked upon as guilty unless proven innocent, despite pious principles to the contrary. Morality was to be the highest aspiration of a child even if he was too young to put such a label on the system of his teaching. It was an artificial code of conduct that allowed no dissent or argument. Morality in teaching demanded the 'moral': the lesson behind the simple tales that had been devised to make the child believe that he was being entertained whilst he was being instructed. Idleness was not merely stasis but the road to Damnation. Improvement, which meant recognition of one's errors and their avoidance, came through learning of the misfortunes of the wicked and the rewards of the righteous.

Nursery books in the first half of the nineteenth century were instruments for elevating the mind rather than for making the heart beat a little faster. Every title had an explanatory sub-title revealing to the satisfaction of the parent and the dismay of the child the particular flavour of the

medicine to be found between the covers. *The Fat Cat or Do Not Ask for All You See (All in Words of No More than Three Letters)*, published by Dean's in the 1840s, was one of the more benign examples. Children's books written purely for entertainment were uncommon. Fiction was non-truth and, as such, was immoral. Fairy tales existed but were looked upon as frivolous and disruptive to Improvement.

The level of tuition for the inmates of the nursery, when not conducive towards precociousness, must have been baffling and frustrating to the

C4 (opposite left) Metal money-box, 'The Hod Carrier', from the Mason Bank Excelsior series, USA, 1887; height 7½ in. Museum of Childhood, Edinburgh.

C5 (opposite right) Dolls' house, *c.* 1870. Granville, Ohio. Carved and painted wood, glass and paper; height 38 in., width 36 in., depth 36 in. Collection of Lorna Lieberman.

C6 (opposite below) Noah's Ark, painted wood, *c.* 1860. Height 7 in., length 11 in. Museum of Childhood, Edinburgh.

30 (left) 'Wee Agness' bank, 1906; height 6 in. Museum of Childhood, Edinburgh.

31 (below left) 'Always did 'spise a mule' money box, cast metal, 1897. J. & E. Stevens & Co., USA. Museum of Childhood, Edinburgh.

32 (above) Money box, Buckley ware, *c.* 1870. Grosvenor Museum, Chester.

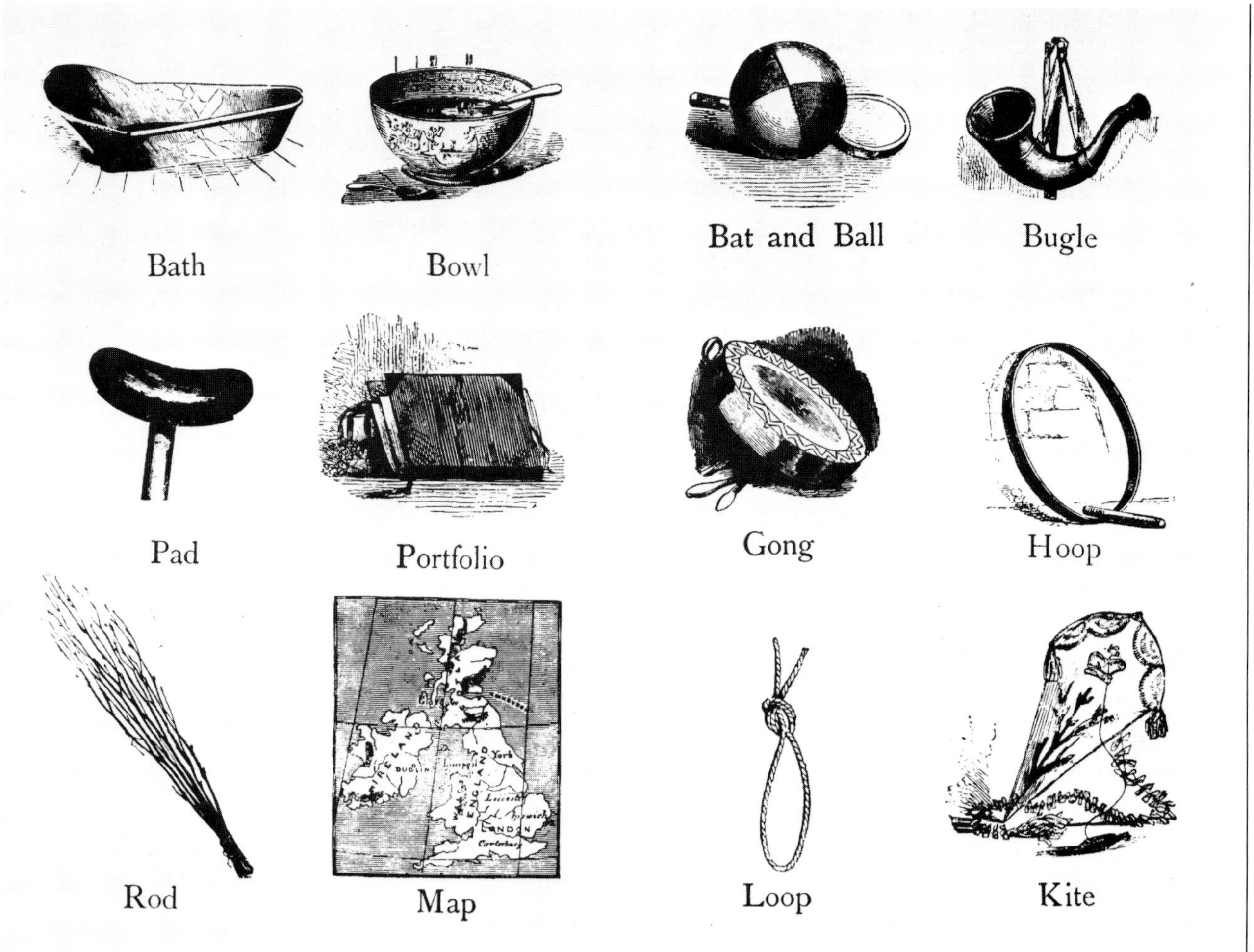

33 Illustrations from *Little Emily's Book of Common Objects*, compiled by Mrs Goode, *c.* 1880.

less intelligent. In the Annual volume for 1833 of *The Nursery Magazine*, each month was headed enticingly with the name of a metal. 'October', for example, began with 'LEAD', illustrated by a woodcut of a Gentleman shooting snipe with his little lead bullets, after which followed a discussion of the metal, its sources, its extraction and its uses. The sections for December included 'The Ill-spent Hours'; 'Lectures on the Old Testament'; 'Master Simplicity's Happy Home' ('... when Mr Self-Conceit was gone, Mr Humble-Mind made haste to go back to Master Simplicity and tell him the good news ...'); 'History and Geography' ('Buonapart was a wonderful man, he was very clever but did not care what he did to get power. He had no religion, as far as we know at least ...'); 'The Economy of Nature', and a poem: 'Against Pride in Dress' ('Angels are happy clothed in wings, But our new clothes are dangerous things, The child well dressed had need beware, Lest his fine raiment prove a snare ...').

Any child who underwent such an upbringing would have been hard put in life to undo either the priggishness or rebelliousness that must have been induced in him. Children were sacrificial objects on the altar of didacticism, their ashes scattered about the feet of the God of Truth. Their happiness was based on the fact that, surrounded as they were by siblings and contemporaries, they had not lost the art of play. Toys were plentiful and inventive, and dolls and dolls' houses for girls and soldiers and forts for boys, with Noah's Arks as shared delights were then, as always, the basic inspiration for the imaginative flights of fancy that were the essence of play (C5), (C6). With books, though, little excuse was needed for some authors and illustrators to indulge, under the name of Right Behaviour, in sadistic portrayal of the torments that awaited the unruly, or even the unwary, child. Cautionary tales were accepted forms of story telling. *The First Chapter of Accidents* and *Remarkable Events Containing Caution and Instruction for Children* were early nineteenth-century collections of horror stories. The tales told of little boys who had their eyes put out through not looking where they were going (into a crate carried by a porter), or of being dragged off by the leg by a savage dog as a retribution for disobedience, each story being suitably illustrated with realistic woodcuts.

The style was puffed up to magnificent proportions in Heinrich Hoffman's *Struwwelpeter* with its attractive sub-title of 'Pretty Stories and Funny Pictures for Little Children', possibly one of the most deceptive lures ever devised for the unsuspecting child. Verses of the order of those in 'The Story of Little Suck-a-thumb' in which we find the notorious 'Snip! Snap! Snip! the scissors go;/And Conrad cries out Oh!, Oh!, Oh!/ Snip! Snap! Snip! They go so fast,/That both his thumbs are off at last' (34), make one wonder at the chthonic demonic forces within us that have made *Struwwelpeter* the best-selling nursery book of all time.

Threats were plentiful, and illustrators were often ready to seize on the more stimulating aspects of a story to give zest to their work. Threats of abandonment were used: 'The witch will come and get you' is only another way of saying 'Mama will stop loving you, will leave you, and a Bad Mama will come in her place'. Threats of location were used, ranging from 'The Industrial School', as such places of juvenile correction were called in former days, to Hell itself: both of them extensions of the loss of the beautiful home. Threats of servitude or of the imposition of menial tasks, as with Cinderella, were those of loss of a favoured position in the family. The sadistic elements in children's books were carefully masked by the moral tones in which they were presented. Only when overt moral teaching became unfashionable did there come to an end this hypocrisy of promoting fear in the name of offering enlightenment. By the late nineteenth century nursery literature had come to stress the more positive aspects of good behaviour and emphasize the rewards that good deeds and right thinking would bring. Patronization of the aged, the sick and the lower orders, or a combination of all three was sometimes inevitable but

The door flew open, in he ran,
The great, long, red-legg'd scissor-man.
Oh! children, see! the tailor s come
And caught out little Suck-a-Thumb.
Snip! Snap! Snip! the scissors go;
And Conrad cries out—Oh! Oh! Oh!
Snip! Snap! Snip! They go so fast,
That both his thumbs are off at last.
Mamma comes home; there Conrad stands,
And looks quite sad, and shows his hands;—
"Ah!" said Mamma, "I knew he'd come
To naughty little Suck-a-Thumb."
(16)

34 Heinrich Hoffman: *The English Struwwelpeter*, Griffith, Farran, Browne, London, 1848.

it was, one would suppose, an improvement on Struwwelpeter (C7).

All protoplasm requires stimulus for survival. When the stimulus is uncontrolled the result is trauma. The dividing line between the two is a fine one, with safety on one side and danger on the other. Resilience varies in the child as it does in the adult. The threshold of tolerance differs from person to person, and the child who has nightmares over *Struwwelpeter* might have no terrors from the mayhem in *Jack the Giant Killer*. There is no universal scale of resilience. It is impossible to determine just how much stimulus is a good thing; how much delights the child, or to what extent he should be sheltered from threatening images. In compensation though, time provides a levelling out, for the capacity to accommodate increases with age as developing experience teaches the child more possible ways of resolving the conflict.

Even then, anything of a potentially terrifying nature is acceptable only if it is reversible: that is to say, only if some form of redemption takes place. Making the child aware that terror exists could, conceivably, be of some benefit, provided that he is allowed to look on from a position of safety, and is never left to feel that he has been abandoned to it. It is a dangerous experiment but it has merits. A metaphorical puddle-testing, the stepping from a place of safety into the unknown without actually relinquishing the ties to a base, yet knowing all the time that he is loved and secure, is important to the child. But there must be no undue prolongation of horror.

Happiness is the resolution of conflict. This is why so often in play the child cries out 'Again!'. The child who has had his face splashed with water will laugh, but the one who has had his face pushed below the surface is terrified. Peter Hollindale expresses it well in his *Choosing Books for Children* (Paul Elek, 1974). In a phrase referring to the text of children's books, but applying equally well to the illustrations, he wrote: 'It is not the function of books to put out the stars and take the compass away'. 'Peek-a-boo' is fine and fun. Dressing up in strange clothes to make the child uncertain for the moment is a game, as long as the child knows that in the end his bewilderment is going to be resolved. The story of Jack and the Beanstalk is no more than the chase game, with the happy ending of reaching safety, home and mama. The child in the nursery should never be allowed to cross into monster-land without a return ticket.

Nursery stories are able to break the rule that good should triumph and the wicked witch die. Illustrations, on the other hand, are frozen moments: stills from the animated story of the action, and can easily leave the child with an image that is potentially traumatic. In order to play the game correctly, the pictures should alienate the child from the place or the character featured and always allow him to step back from the action to make judgments in his own terms. Threats can be dissipated by resorting to disguise, with the hero as a clown or doll, or a child from another land:

a device which Helen Bannerman, for example, uses in her *Little Black Sambo* of 1899. Despite the callousness of the tale, with its carnivorous tigers centrifuged into butter and eaten with pancakes, and its arrogant insensitivity, so typical of its time, whereby Sambo's parents are portrayed as the risible 'Black Jumbo' and 'Black Mambo' (and this in India), Sambo himself is really an alienation disguise for his little readers.

Far better and safer is the parodic device of anthropomorphism. Make your hero an animal and you can get away with far more dangerous situations. Yet, even here, some caution is needed, for too realistic a metamorphosis, as in Rupert Bear, where the character is nothing more than a human being with an animal's head, and where the situations are feasible ones of the local village and other familiar surroundings, has been known to cause fear of a possible real-life encounter with just such a para-human, no matter how nice-natured he might be.

Of all the illustrations that have been made for the nursery, none have been more frightening than those drawn in 1862 by Gustav Doré for an edition of Perrault's *Fairy Tales*. It was possibly the first time that the Gothic-Romantic style had been used for children's illustrations and the results were undeniably horrifying. The stories themselves were not always the most serene, and the illustrations were made more menacing by being given an unrelieved black density, with the characters drawn in looming close-up (35), (36). The realism was silent and frightening because the artist had focussed attention on the horrific elements. The

35 Gustave Doré: 'Hop-o'-my-Thumb' from *Perrault, Contes*, 1861.

sharp curved claws and teeth of 'Puss in Boots', and the dead mice hanging from his belt, are pointers by the artist as deliberate as the more obvious one of the knife at the throat of the children in 'Petit Poucet' ('Hop-o'-my-Thumb').

36 (opposite) Gustave Doré: 'Puss in Boots' from *Perrault, Contes*, 1861.

37 Howard Pyle, *The Wonder Clock*, Harper & Bros, 1887.

The actual type of stimulus needed to produce terror in children varies widely. For one correspondent the sausage in Howard Pyle's *The Wonder Clock*, Freudian explanations notwithstanding, produced nightmares of being eaten alive by a dog (37). Another shared the terrors of Alice in her apparently never-ending fall down the rabbit hole. The late Kenneth Clarke put on record his childhood fear of the all-seeing lumbering trees in Arthur Rackham's illustrations. Like Snow White's apple, many traditional nursery tales, especially the orally transmitted folk tales one finds in Grimm, had venom concealed beneath their attractive surface. The wolf in *The Three Little Pigs* was scalded to death in a pot of boiling water and eaten for supper. 'Tom Thumb', after having triumphed so many times, was eventually killed by an enormous spider and had his blood sucked out.

38 'Jack the Giant Killer', artist unknown, from *Our Darlings*, Shaw & Co., London, 1907.

In the hands of an artist insensitive to the feelings of children, illustrations can be as frightening when they attempt to interpret the text faithfully as when they are made a licence for sadistic indulgence. The 1907 edition of the annual *Our Darlings* – a title evoking milkiness and baby powder – has a rhyming version of *Jack the Giant Killer* with an illustration that, from the staring red eyes of the struggling giant to the heads of his victims hanging from the wall, is unlikely to have allowed any child who had it read as a bedtime story to have pleasant dreams (38). Adventure has ended, and terror remains in its place. There rules the dubious philosophy that Evil has to exist for Good to be properly appreciated.

Many of the illustrations that overstep the bounds of safety are examples of no more than thoughtlessness or misjudgment. A seemingly innocent drawing by Charles Robinson, 'Where the wild flowers are born', done in 1897 for the book *King Longbeard*, portrayed the budding flowers as wide-eyed homunculi (39), and left, inadvertently, sinister undertones for the sensitive child. As with the Doré illustrations they offer no resolution. The border has been crossed and the child abandoned in a foreign land. On the other hand, the illustration by R.F. Bunner in *The Fairy Court* of 1928, with its blatant display of sadism, is inexcusable (40). Equally vicious is a nasty little picture in *The Chummy Book*, an evident misnomer, in which, using the alienation effect, the illustrator tries to show his young white readers the dangers of playing with fire, by callously having two little black children set themselves alight and burn to death. Reality is always difficult to manipulate. A good illustrator can often dispel the terrors by releasing the tension in laughter but, as the *Struwwelpeter* illustrations show, even caricature is not always effective.

A distinction must be made between indulgence in horror and the confrontation of the child with death. In the former, any teasing by the secure adult of the vulnerable child is a sinful misuse of power. Its mockery of those more sensitive in spirit is both a bullying and a form of exhibitionism and, as such, is a cover up for some deficiency. Under the guise of pretending to train the child by the presentation of fictional nightmares, it treats actual nightmares with an insensitivity and high-minded disdain that the trainers always seem incapable of applying to their own exercises.

The nineteenth-century attitude towards death, though, was different from today's. Loss of a sibling or a parent (hence the many stories of orphaned children) was an experience that every child knew about from an early age. Black mourning bands encircled tiny arms and black ribbons fluttered from little nursery hats as pennants signalling to the world that the players in a solemn tragedy had arrived. Death was common in any large family but was cushioned in the child by the comforting presence of a number of brothers and sisters, as well as by the stress laid on the privileges of Heaven. Illness was much more closely associated with death. It was an age of nostrums and patent medicines. Advertising, like teaching,

39 (opposite) Charles Robinson: 'Where the Baby Flowers are Born', from *King Longbeard* by B. MacGregor, John Lane, 1897.

WHERE THE BABY FLOWERS ARE BORN,

40 R.F. Bunner: 'Judgment of Solomon', from *The Fairy Court* by B.H. Nadal, Arundel Press, New York, 1928.

was direct and intended to shock. 'DO NOT UNTIMELY DIE' cautioned an advertisement for Fennings Fever Cure in *Our Nursery Book* of 1900. 'DON'T LET YOUR CHILD DIE' warned another in *Our Little Dot's Annual* for 1897. For any fever the accepted treatment, which now would take the form of aspirin or a course of antibiotics, was a week or two in bed. During part of each year the child would live in a world in which the entrances and exits of the mother or nanny would leave an impression of shadowy, ghostly figures, silent and gliding. Delirium and fantasy combined to make images that belonged half to reality and half to a world of dreams and make-believe, so that what was real and what was read in books merged and blended in a way that gave form to the insubstantial and softened the edges of actuality.

With a measurable portion of the child's life given up to illness, reading was a welcome diversion in the long hours of the nursery. Among those who had the means literacy was high. Stories which, nowadays, would be condemned as unnecessarily morbid related to the child's actual experience. The inquest over Cock Robin, or the funeral procession in the story *Mammy Tittleback and her Family* that the Bostonian Addie Ledyard illustrated in 1881 are by no means horrific in their necrophilia (41). The catafalque and the suitably serious expressions on the faces of the children are intended merely to rouse appropriate feelings of compassion in little readers, not to shock them. Fear of illustrations in nursery books takes many forms and, while pictures that frighten unintentionally are to be regretted, the deliberate use of horror to gain effect is to be condemned outright.

The child's journey from bassinet to full-sized bed was not one of simple progress and natural growth but one of false signposts and unforeseen hazards, where chance played a large part, and traps of ignorance, superstition and disease were ever present. The fact that so many triumphed is testimony to the resilience of the species rather than the soundness of the principles of its nurture.

41 Illustration by Addie Ledyard, from *Mammy Tittleback and her Family* by 'H.H.', Roberts Bros., Boston, 1881.

CHAPTER 4

Crockery and Wallpaper

The Victorian obsession with the importance of correct training extended, somewhat unpredictably, beyond the pages of nursery books to the surfaces of children's crockery. These offered an advantage over books in that, not only was there the incentive to look for nanny's approval shining from every cleanly scraped bowl, but they also permitted a dose of moral principles to be measured out to the child three times a day with meals.

Up to the middle of the nineteenth century children used the same dinner or tea services as their parents, and the miniature china with which children played 'House' had the same patterns as the family ware (42). By the 1850s, manufacturers, seeing in the nursery a potential market, were beginning to produce cups, plates, bowls and mugs decorated with themes related to children. A plate of that period illustrating Joseph's second dream, with Joseph given a patterned coverlet and what appears to be a bedside chair, was an early example of decorativeness combining with utility to offer nourishment for both body and soul (43). Plates and, more especially, mugs, were used to convey words or maxims of an exhortatory nature: 'Never Speak to Deceive nor Listen to Betray' was typical. Mugs were decorated with scenes illustrating 'Charity', 'Industry' or 'Generosity' (44). A 'Reward of Merit' series existed demonstrating in a dignified and often symbolic manner the recognition of the type of obedience expected from the child. The decoration of the 'Diligence' mug (45), for example, would be recognized by all who received it as illustrating the lines by the Reverend Isaac Watts 'How doth the little busy bee Improve each shining hour'.

More sobering thoughts were expressed by a plate (46), whose centre

42 (above) 'Nursery Tea', Bradford Art Galleries and Museums.

43 (left) Nursery plate: 'Joseph and his Brethren', *c.* 1860. Collection of Pauline Flick.

44 (below) Nursery mug: 'Charity', *c.* 1850. Brighton Museum & Art Gallery.

45 (below) Nursery mug: 'Diligence', *c.* 1850. Brighton Museum & Art Gallery.

46 (below) Nursery plate: 'The tulip and the butterfly', *c.* 1850. Collection of Pauline Flick.

47 (opposite) John Constable: original watercolour on the title page of *Songs Divine and Moral* by Isaac Watts, 1833. Victoria & Albert Museum.

picture, surrounded by a pretty border in relief of daisies, was based on an actual watercolour done in 1833 by John Constable in a copy of Watts' *Songs, Divine and Moral*: a standard children's primer of the eighteenth century that the artist had presented to his daughter. The designer of the plate was aware of the need to adapt Constable's drawing to the requirements of the circular format. He introduced a hollyhock on the left, graded in size the railings on the right, and set the text in an arc. The resulting picture was much cruder than the original but was far more balanced as a pattern (47).

The tulip and the butterfly
Appear in gayer coats than I.
Let me be dress'd fine as I will.
Flies worms and flowers exceed me still.

SONGS,

DIVINE AND MORAL,

FOR

THE USE OF CHILDREN.

BY THE

REV. ISAAC WATTS, D.D.

Much of the everyday crockery that was used in both Britain and the United States was manufactured in the Potteries, and earthenware made there with decorations varying from frolicsome cherubs to characters from Dickens and scenes from *Uncle Tom's Cabin* sold equally well in both countries (48). Children's china, larger than dolls' china and intended for play, was in use for nursery teas by the middle of the century. Within a short time, household china in smaller sizes, with designs intended specifically for children, was being produced in the fashionable colours of pink, green, lavender and, most commonly, blue (49). A special 'Flow Blue', where the colour had run, was exported to the United States where its mistiness, to the delight of its British manufacturers who had thought that the initial wrongly baked batch was going to prove a financial disaster, turned out to be the most popular colour of all. Mass-produced nursery ware was generally monochromatic, but one could buy exquisite examples of multi-coloured hand-painted china of the quality of the Filey China mug (C8): one of a series of six, each showing a different farmyard animal in an appropriate setting.

By the beginning of the twentieth century many firms had in their catalogues not only children's tableware but other items of pottery specifically intended for the nursery. Doulton, for example, had marketed an especially beautiful tea service decorated by W. Savage Cooper with scenes from nursery rhymes (50), while another, by an undeservedly anonymous designer, carried a new series of illustrations for 'Alice in

48 (below) Nursery plate: 'Uncle Tom's Cabin', *c.* 1860. Gladstone Pottery Museum, Stoke-on-Trent.

49 (right) Nursery teapot: 'Cinderella', *c.* 1870. Collection of Pauline Flick.

Wonderland' (51). In addition, the company manufactured water filters with Noah's Ark and the animals in relief (52), for the purification of the, as yet, unsafe water from the reservoirs. Pottery candlesticks could be bought with designs by John Hassall, and a green stoneware hot water bottle was made especially for the nursery with the word 'Baby' and little animals embossed on the side (53). All these items, though, were simple fare compared with the beautifully detailed night lights that the Staffordshire Potteries started to manufacture not many years later. These, in the

50 (below) Nursery tea set: 'Nursery Rhymes', designed by William Savage Cooper for Doulton, 1906.

51 (bottom) Nursery tea service: 'Alice in Wonderland', by an unknown designer for Doulton, 1906.

DOULTON & CO. LIMITED, LAMBETH, LONDON, S.E.

DOULTON'S GERM-PROOF FILTERS

DINING ROOM AND NURSERY PATTERNS.

FIGURE 68.

FIGURE 72

FIGURE 69.

THE above are in the well-known decorated salt-glazed stoneware, and are eminently suited to Dining Room and Nursery use. As in the case of the foregoing filters they are fitted with the screw attachment Germ-proof Tubes. They are highly decorative in appearance, and no point of utility is sacrificed. The Nursery, or Noah's Ark, Pattern is one which particularly appeals to children.

PRICES.

	Fig. 68.	Fig. 69.	Fig. 72.	Fig. 73.*	
Size	2	3	2	2	gallons.
Price	47/6	67/6	50/-	45/-	each.
Overall Dimensions:					
Height	22	23	21	21	inches.
Diameter	9	10	8	8	inches.
Weight	25	36	23	22	lbs.
Quantity that will pack in one Tierce, charged 6/- ...	9	8	9	9	

* As Fig. 72, but in brown stoneware with white figures.

Extra Tubes, 3/6 each.

form of elaborate fairy tale cottages, had a hollow at the back in which a candle could be inserted that would make the windows glow in a way such as to give reassurance to the most nervous child (c9).

A number of children's illustrators, including Jessie M. King in Scotland and Pixie O'Harris in Australia, painted nursery china, both for their own use and for sale. Jessie M. King had the biscuit ware sent up from the actual potteries to her home in Kirkcudbright and would paint mugs, bowls, cups, saucers and plates in bright colours supplied by the pottery people themselves. Both inner and outer surfaces were given enchanting decorations of flowers, children at play and, above all, rabbits. The base of each article was further decorated with a green gate (relating to her house 'The Greengate'), her initials and the inevitable rabbit (54). The pottery was then packed up in the crates again and sent back for firing.

Favourite children's characters began to appear on nursery ware. In addition to Alice china, complete tea services were decorated with figures taken from Kate Greenaway's illustrations (55) and, before long, the Beatrix Potter books (130). In the 1900s Cecil Aldin designed nursery plates that used his famous mongrel dog as a motif, and in 1926 Mabel Lucie Attwell designed a tea set that featured her little elves the 'Boo-Boos'. The milk jug was in the shape of a 'Boo-Boo' saluting, the teapot was a cottage with a small green 'Boo-Boo' standing in the doorway, while the sugar basin was an attractive spotted Fly Agaric, fatal to any child who might have been encouraged by the sweetness of sugar to try the real mushroom – a particularly disturbing thought in that the range was used by the Royal Princesses in the early 1930s and received a great deal of

52 (opposite) Doulton's 'Germ-proof Filters', *c.* 1905.

53 (below left) Nursery hot water bottle, green stoneware, Doulton, *c.* 1910.

54 Jessie M. King: design mark on nursery teacup, *c.* 1936.

55 Nursery tea service, designed after Kate Greenaway, date unknown. Collection of Pauline Flick.

56 Nursery tableware: 'Paddington Bear', designed and manufactured by the Coalport Division of Wedgwood, 1976. © Paddington and Co. Ltd.

publicity at the time (C10). Many other individual characters from children's fiction have appeared on nursery china in both the United States and Great Britain. 'Uncle Wiggily', Howard Garis's gentlemanly and wholly American rabbit; 'Felix the Cat'; 'Thelwell children', on or off their ponies; 'Paddington Bear' (56); the Disney animals; 'The Muppets'; 'Snoopy' and, of course, 'Teddy' (57), have all participated in nursery teas.

The 'twenties and 'thirties were periods of intensive self-searching into the quality of design of manufactured goods, and the more responsible companies were attempting to encourage good design in mass-produced articles. Unfortunately, the artist who could draw attractive pictures was

57 (top left) Nursery plate: 'Teddy Bears', Cetem Ware, *c.* 1912. Museum of Childhood, Edinburgh.

58 (top right) Nursery tea service: 'The Wireless', Heathcote China, *c.* 1929. Collection of Pauline Flick.

59 (above) Nursery tea service: 'The Children's Future', Lawley, 1930. Collection of Pauline Flick.

not necessarily one who had the ability to produce a suitable decoration for the rounded surface of a cup or a plate. The 'Wireless' tea set that Heathcote china commissioned in 1929 captured the excitement of the novelty of radio but was cluttered as a design (58). Lawley's 'The Children's Future' tea service of 1930 was better in design but here, because of the attempt to manufacture a set with a modernistic shape, each surface had the effect of being treated like a page in a book: something that the carrying of the verse round the corner of the sugar bowl did not wholly overcome (59). Best of all was a Doulton's 'Nursery Rhyme' tea set of 1920 in which both the 'Simple Simon' plate and the 'Oranges and Lemons' saucer were designed with great understanding of both surface

60 Nursery tea service: 'Simple Simon', Royal Doulton Tableware Ltd., 1920. Collection of Pauline Flick.

61 Nursery tea service, designed by Miriam Wornum for Ashtead Potters Ltd., 1932.

62 'Nurseryware for the Discriminating Juvenile', designed by Susie Cooper for Wedgwood, *c.* 1936.

and form, not only in the decorativeness of the groups of figures but also in their imaginative placing against the white ground of the china (60).

During the 1930s many pottery manufacturers and designers - Miriam Wornum for Ashtead Potters and Susie Cooper for both her own independent company and for Wedgwood's 'Nurseryware for the Discriminating Juvenile' - produced particularly modern well-designed nursery china (61), (62). Eric Ravilious's alphabet set of 1937 for Wedgwood was particularly outstanding. Plates and mugs for teaching children their letters or how to tell the time, had been in use well before the turn of the century (63). The most common arrangement had been to have the alphabet set round the rim of the plate with a picture of animals or children at

63 (below left) Alphabet Plate, 1882. Browngill's Pottery Company, Tunstall. City Museum and Art Gallery, Stoke-on-Trent.

64 (above) Nursery mug, designed by Eric Ravilious for Wedgwood, 1937.

play in the centre. Occasionally more imaginative designers would see the plate as a complete surface for decoration, and design the alphabet in a wedge or crescent shape, with the illustration occupying the 'dark' side. Ravilious's design was both beautiful and dignified, with each letter accompanied by a little illustration. It provided its own original solution to the even more difficult problem of how to set such a quantity of information around the small cylindrical surface of a drinking mug (64).

Today's alphabet plates, like the alphabet books, are the innocuous survivors of the practice of using nursery objects as vehicles for the dissemination of good moral principles. Given the disciplines of the times,

C7 (opposite) Nursery picture, *A Kindly Act*, 1904. Chromolithograph printed in Holland.

C8 (overleaf, above left) Pottery mug, 'Child and Lamb', manufactured by Filey China; hand-painted *c.* 1890. Collection Pauline Flick.

C9 (overleaf, above right) Night light, Staffordshire Potteries, *c.* 1930. Height $5\frac{1}{2}$ in. Museum of Childhood, Edinburgh.

C10 (overleaf, below) Nursery tea set, 'The Boo-Boos', designed by Mabel Lucie Attwell, 1926; manufactured by the Shelley Pottery. Plate 7 in. diameter, teapot $4\frac{1}{4}$ in. height. Museum of Childhood, Edinburgh. © Lucie Attwell Ltd.

C11 (overleaf, right) Nursery wallpaper, 'The Toys', France, *c.* 1870. Cooper-Hewitt Museum, New York.

the Victorians' attitude was understandable: 'Waste not, want not' applied to food for the mind as well as for the body. What is surprising is the forebearance of the Victorians to use, after its introduction into the nursery in the 1850s, the eminently suitable surface of wallpaper for the promotion of these ideals, and yet, from the very outset, nursery wallpaper was used only decoratively and never for didactic purposes.

65 Nursery wallpaper: 'Robinson Crusoe', manufactured in the USA, *c.* 1850. Cooper-Hewitt Museum, New York.

The first nursery papers, although printed in single colours, had ambitious designs. The patterns were usually composed of a series of narrative pictures, each with a group of figures in their own localized scenery, and captioned like a book of illustrations. The effect, as in an American wallpaper of the 1850s with scenes from *Robinson Crusoe*, was similar to a panel of tiles but in the more intelligently designed papers the space around each illustration was cleverly used to avoid the feel of crowding or formal severity (65). A richly coloured French paper of the 1870s had a design that was far better integrated and better printed than anything to be found at that time in Great Britain (C11). It was spoilt by the claustrophobic oppressiveness of its somewhat nightmarish toys but, nevertheless, it had a flow which a more formal contemporary British paper, with its design of nursery rhymes lacked. Even so, the British wallpaper was far more suited to its purpose because the artist understood the importance of simplicity for the presentation of his message (C12). Despite the crudity of the drawing, the elimination of non-essentials in the scenes and the fact that the paper was available in several colour combinations made it a popular one for Victorian nurseries.

It was not, however, until the more adventurous papers with patterns

LOOK AT THIS WEE, JOLLY ELF –
FIDO CAUGHT IT – ALL HIMSELF!
MABEL LUCIE ATTWELL
A FAIRY BOAT
TO TAKE US AWAY
TO THE LAND: WHERE
THE MERMAIDS LOVE TO PLAY.
MABEL LUCIE ATTWELL

BOYS & GIRLS COME OUT TO PLAY.
THREE CHILDREN WENT A SLIDING.
& IT CAN'T SEE.
HE BEGGARS ARE COMING TO TOWN.
THE CAT'S IN THE

based on illustrations by Walter Crane and Kate Greenaway were manufactured that well-designed and sympathetic children's wallpaper came to the nursery. It was appreciated that the walls of the nursery were unsuitable for the sombre-coloured, heavily patterned wallpapers that William Morris recommended for the living-room. Even when the Morris influence invaded the nursery, its exponents Crane and, later, Charles Voysey ensured that any density of pattern was lessened by the use of light pastel colours. But the art of wallpaper design was the art of organizing space. The artist who could negotiate the difficulties of what was to happen in between the units that made up the pattern, as Crane did in his reticulated design for 'The House that Jack Built' (66), had mastered the art of wallpaper design. Similarly, in a wallpaper 'The Months', which used themes from Kate Greenaway's *Almanac for 1893*, the pattern was built up of what were, in their original form, single-page plates in tiny books and transformed by the delicate use of chains of flowers and foliage into a delightfully continuous whole (67).

Spielman and Layard, in their biography of Kate Greenaway, described how she sold some of her drawings from both her *Birthday Book* and her

C12 (opposite above) Nursery wallpaper, 'British Nursery Songs', *c.* 1890. Private collection.

C13 (opposite below) Nursery frieze, 'The Sea Shore', designed by Will Owen 1912. Whitworth Art Gallery, Manchester.

66 (below left) Nursery wallpaper: 'The House that Jack Built', designed by Walter Crane, 1886. Victoria & Albert Museum.

67 (below right) Nursery wallpaper: 'The Months', designed after Kate Greenaway, *c.* 1894. Whitworth Art Gallery, Manchester.

68 Nursery wallpaper: 'A Frog He Would a-Wooing Go', designed by Walter Crane for Jeffrey & Co., 1877. Victoria & Albert Museum.

Almanacs, with exclusive rights of reproduction as 'sanitary wallpapers', to Walker's of Middleton, near Manchester. Kate Greenaway never designed specifically for wallpaper, and what are referred to as 'Kate Greenaway Wallpapers' are all sensitively organized wall-charts of her book illustrations. Between 1875 and 1906, on the other hand, Jeffries and Co. manufactured seven papers to original designs by Walter Crane that were the finest children's wallpapers so far produced. Without actually copying any of the illustrations from his *Toy Books*, Crane drew fresh interpretations of the characters he had used and linked them imaginatively by colour, line and the skilful use of vignettes and tiny incidental decorations. An eighth paper, of nursery rhyme characters, each one separated from its neighbours by a very Greenaway-style lacework of flowering branches, was printed in an exclusive edition for the nursery at Castle Howard in Yorkshire.

Each of Crane's papers was unique in design, and his approach towards these designs varied throughout the range. In the 'Humpty Dumpty' paper of 1876 the themes were those of *The Baby's Opera*, but the drawings were new, as was the scrollwork and lettering with which he unified the elements. The paper 'A Frog He Would a-Wooing Go' of 1877, which was also adapted from two of the songs in *The Baby's Opera*, had the appearance of a panel of decorated tiles, with froggy incidents alternating with square patterns of stylized flowers (68). In 'The House that Jack Built', perhaps the most imaginative of all his nursery wallpapers, the bells, the rampant roosters and the last flick of the cat's tail, were just some of the delightful touches of invention that Crane introduced to relieve the formality of the pattern (66). In two of the papers he parodied the style of William Morris, his mentor. In 'The Fairy Garden' of 1890, for which he used ideas from his book *Flora's Feast*, he transformed Morris's dank acanthus leaves into a brilliant yellow incandescence of fairies. Even more ingeniously, in the 'Sleeping Beauty' paper of 1879, the overall pattern of foliage, so beloved of Morris, became the thicket of brambles which surrounded the sleeping court (69).

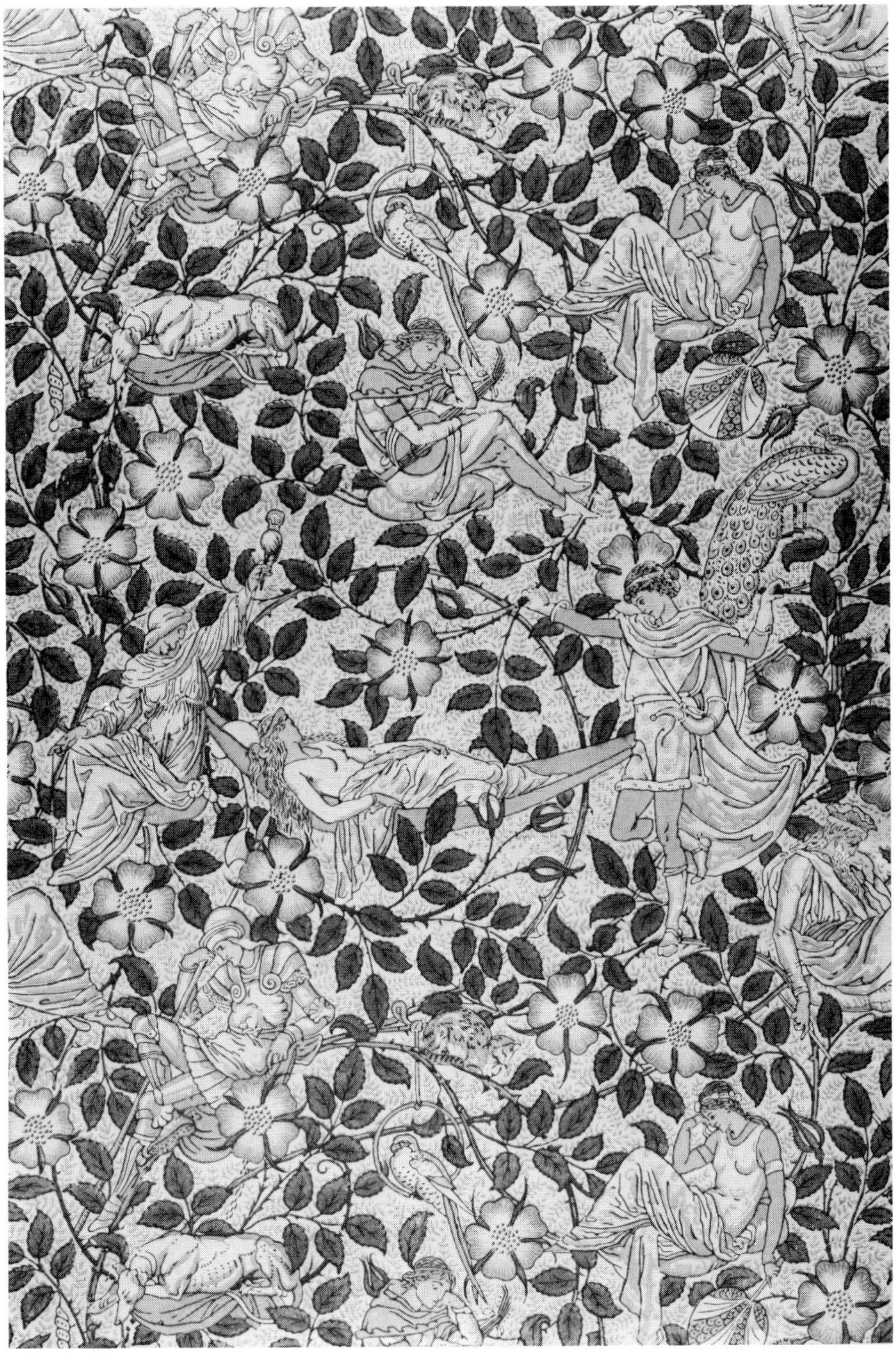

69 Nursery wallpaper: 'The Sleeping Beauty', designed by Walter Crane for Jeffrey & Co., 1879. Victoria & Albert Museum.

70 (above) Nursery wallpaper: 'Nursery Rhymes', after Walter Crane, USA, *c.* 1890. Cooper-Hewitt Museum, New York.

71 (right) Walter Crane: 'Little Bo-Peep', from *The Baby's Opera*, Routledge & Sons, 1887.

The Crane and Greenaway wallpapers were as popular in New York as in London. The United States at that time did not subscribe to any international copyright agreement, and one could find there locally made copies of original Crane and Greenaway papers as well as unauthorized ones made up of illustrations taken directly from the picture books (70), (71). 'The Months', designed and printed in the United States, and very close in likeness to Kate Greenaway's original could be bought from any supplier. Different flowers linked the vignettes and there were minor differences in some of the pictures, but the copy was a good one and a purchaser would not be aware of the differences (67), (72).

Wallpaper friezes, usually mounted against a plain background, came into fashion for the nursery during the 1890s, and were both decorative

72 Nursery wallpaper: 'The Months', after Kate Greenaway, USA, after 1894. Cooper-Hewitt Museum, New York.

and economical. Because the question of 'sequence' came into the idea of a pictorial frieze, narrative material was especially suitable, and many of the most successful friezes were done by book illustrators. Kate Greenaway's 'Processions', as she called them - her troupes of Pre-Raphaelite maidens dressed with diaphanous insubstantiality, bearing garlands and fruit, and usually marking their measured progress with the play of their timbrels, were ideal for use in this way. The illustrators Cecil Aldin and John Hassall, both separately and jointly, designed a number of friezes around the turn of the century. These were based on nursery rhymes: a form sufficiently concise to let a complete narrative be presented within a relatively short format. Hassall had the cartoonist's ability to eliminate all but the essentials in his illustrations. The uniformly solid outline he gave his figures and his use of flat bright colour had made him an outstanding poster artist with an instantly recognizable style that was ideal for work on friezes. He designed many decorations for nursery walls independently of Aldin and, in addition to friezes of toys, dolls, Noah's Arks and nursery rhymes, he designed vertical panels to be used in conjunction with the friezes in order to allow a relief from the horizontal line. Some of the panels were done in series. One group, for example, called 'Times of the Day', showed children at 'Play Time', 'Lesson Time' and 'Bed Time' (73). Another series of 'Flower Dances' showed children acting out those nursery games: 'Ring O'Roses' or 'Buttercups and Daisies', that had flowers in their titles. A third set, 'Morning', 'Noon' and 'Night' was given the honour of being purchased for the nurseries of both the Dutch and Spanish Royal Families (74).

Hassall's influence was considerable, and his followers, Will Owen and Mabel Lucie Attwell, also produced papers for the nursery. Owen, a Punch cartoonist who was later to achieve fame as the creator of the Bisto Kids, had designed a frieze of 'The House that Jack Built' in 1910 that, in both its lettering and pictorial style, owed much to Walter Crane's refined nursery books. Two years later, however, in a frieze 'The Sea Shore', Hassall's bold imagery could be seen in Owen's work (C13). The characterization was coarser than before, but had a new directness, with the figures drawn with the same rumbustious exaggeration that Hassall used to bring the art of comic papers to nursery walls, and Owen's striking blues ensured that the frieze would liven up the gloomiest nursery days.

Mabel Lucie Attwell, in a 'Nursery Rhyme' frieze of about 1910 showed her own indebtedness to Hassall in the simplicity of her forms and the clever placing of her figures. The sugarloaf hats of soft felt, with the band low down on the brim, were features taken from Hassall's little men. But, in addition, there could already be seen the typical characteristics of Mabel Lucie Attwell's later style in the chubby cheeks and tiny mouths of her children, with the round circles for eyes that gave them the coyness which she was to make so endearing (75).

73 John Hassall: nursery panels, *c.* 1899.

74 Nursery decorated by John Hassall and Cecil Aldin, furnishings by Storey & Co., *c.* 1903.

C14 Nursery picture, *The Lord Watches*, chromolithograph, published by Seitz Wandsbeck, Bavaria, *c.* 1880.

The art of the frieze was the art of being able to make the viewer follow the unfolding of the message. The two most common ways of solving the problem were a circus procession and a line of animals entering the Ark. More unusual and far more subtle was a frieze entitled 'Christopher Robin at the North Pole' made in 1929 after Ernest Shepard's drawings for the Pooh books (76). Here the figures were kept to a minimum, and the eye was compelled to follow the picture round the walls, searching the frozen wastes for the little verticals that relieved the seemingly interminable horizontals. Perhaps the most original solution, though, was devised by Heath Robinson in 1930 for the nursery of the liner *Empress of Britain* (77). His idea was simple. Along the top of the nursery wall the artist painted people running. Men, women and children, young and old, tall

75 Nursery frieze: 'Scenes from Nursery Tales', designed by Mabel Lucie Attwell for Potter, *c.* 1910. Victoria & Albert Museum.

76 Nursery frieze: 'Winnie the Pooh', after Ernest Shepard, *c.* 1929. Cooper-Hewitt Museum, New York.

and short, fat and thin, each one dressed in that parody of the Edwardian style that Heath Robinson made his own, all ran round the room after one another in one long circuitous line. It was a merry-go-round of people, each one having to chase and be chased, none of them knowing why, with the last person, whichever one he or she might have been, running after the first, to complete an ever-moving circle.

JESSIE WILLCOX Smith.

Although nursery wallpapers rarely attempted to be other than decorative, many of the pictures that hung on the walls of Victorian nurseries were as much purposeful as ornamental. Their subjects were usually narrative and, reproductions of Old Masters apart, they were often chosen more for the sentiments they expressed than for their artistic qualities.

C15 Jessie Wilcox Smith: 'Mrs Doasyouwouldbedoneby', from *The Water Babies* by Charles Kingsley. Watercolour for the edition published by Dodd Mead, New York, 1916, and Hodder & Stoughton, London. The Library of Congress, Washington.

77 Nursery frieze, designed by W. Heath Robinson for *The Empress of Britain*, 1930.

The young lancer, echoing in his wild ride the feats of the Saint George in the medallion behind him, expressed the national pride in the glorious achievements of the British army in the Crimea (78). Religious themes abounded and offered reassurances to the child in its exploration of the pitfalls of the world by day or its terrors by night (C14), (79). Pictures of beautiful children being very good, or showing kindness to animals or the aged, were commonplace. They were a crystallization of the hopes of

78 Nursery wall picture: *The Lancer*, artist unknown, *c.* 1865; lithograph. Bradford Art Galleries & Museums.

parents that some of the magic of the picture would imprint itself on their child.

Sentimental art like this – the portrayal of merely the chapter-headings of emotion, based on the irrational generalization that 'whatever is beautiful is, therefore, good' – was not just propaganda for the inmates of the nursery but a measure of current feeling about both artistic and social acceptance. The picturing of white-haired benevolence in *Visiting Grandmamma* (80) was as much an exaggeration of serenity as Mannerism in late-Renaissance painting had become an exaggeration of pose. Grandmas are nice. They are generally wiser than parents. They are more tolerant and have usually learnt that it is often better to do nothing in a situation out of their control. As a picture, *Visiting Grandmamma* is immediately understood, safe, satisfying and unquestionably moral. It is, nevertheless, dishonest as art because its exaggerations are for emotive rather than artistic purposes. The sentiments overwhelm. The picture is, in effect, a piece of pictorial sales talk.

All the ingredients of this sentimental mannerism are to be found in *A Kindly Act* (C7). The idyllic setting of the cottage, the blind farmhand and the beautiful children, are all symbols for tranquillity and goodness. Everything about the picture is designed to promote sympathetic responses in the viewer. The rosy-cheeked, white-haired old man, immaculately clean, is as acceptable a figure to adorn a nursery wall as the equally spotless children: the older one carefully tending the younger as he offers the cup of tea. This picture, like *Visiting Grandmamma*, is bad

79 (above) Nursery wall picture: *Psalm 143*, artist unknown, *c.* 1890; lithograph. Bradford Art Galleries & Museums.

80 (left) Nursery wall picture: *Visiting Grandmamma*, artist unknown, *c.* 1903; steel engraving.

81 Nursery wall picture: *Suspense* by E. Burton Barker for Pears, 1895; lithograph.

art because, in seeking to describe an act of charity, it uses a language that presents its case in histrionic terms and in minutely described detail. It artificially inflates an already dignified message and the result is merely glamorous and far less sincere than, for example, the similar message used as decoration on the 'Charity' mug (44).

Many of the pictures that were found on the nursery walls of late-Victorian homes came from magazines and advertising posters. Periodicals such as *Little Folks* or *Saint Nicholas* regularly included coloured plates for framing. The new art of the poster, especially some of those devised for Pear's soap, also provided many notable nursery decorations (81). The best of these posters, the famous *Bubbles* of Millais became, as a result of what was possibly the cleverest advertising scheme of all time, the most popular of all nursery pictures. It was not, however, until the end of the century, when the publishers Ernest Nister's introduced large-sized versions of some of their book illustrations of dogs and cats in human clothing playing school (82), that pictures were produced which were specifically intended for decorating a nursery in the way that a child himself might have chosen. Even then, for many years, publishers of fine art reproductions felt that nursery pictures were unworthy of their attention. Only in the 1920s did a firm of the calibre of The Medici Society commission its first fairy pictures for hanging in the nursery from the illustrators Margaret W. Tarrant and Millicent Sowerby (83).

Nister's anthropomorphic cats and dogs were the harbingers of fantasy to the nursery walls, but the angelic wonder-children were hard to replace. Fairies and related immortals gained acceptance only gradually, long after

82 Nursery wall picture: *The Cat's Half Holiday*, chromolithograph, Ernest Nister & Sons, *c.* 1890. Museum of Childhood, Edinburgh.

83 (opposite) Nursery wall picture: *Do you believe in Fairies?* by Margaret W. Tarrant, 1922, © The Medici Society Ltd, 1977.

Margaret W. Tarrant

they had become acceptable in children's books (see Chapter 6). When they did come, the fairies were found to be not the spirited hobgoblins of Richard Doyle's *In Fairyland* but a new species that had been waiting at the bottom of the garden with the appearance of little seven-year-old girls dressed, as no self-respecting mothers would ever let their own daughters be dressed, in the flimsiest tulles of an almost immodest shortness.

The fairies, whether of flowers, dells or forest glades, drove away virtually all contenders, other than the ubiquitous Mabel Lucie Attwell children, for a place on the nursery wall. They were the dominant species until the beginning of the Second World War when the harsh realities of the times drove them into exile and they were superseded by the teddy bears and rabbits who were waiting their turn. The new animal pictures: the modern equivalent of the Nister reproductions, retained their popularity, and artists such as Molly Brett, whose early work included book illustrations in the style of the 'fairy school', began to produce pictures teeming with animals and toys pretending to be children (84). The most recent trends have been away from decorating the nursery with special children's art pictures, and falling sales have resulted in a reluctance to risk new designs. Bright inexpensive posters of Disney's or television characters are now common, and Old Master paintings are now coming back to adorn the walls of the children's room, with secular themes instead of the former religious ones. Dürer's 'Hare', as well as replacing the Raphael Madonnas of the nineteenth-century nurseries, has even begun to usurp the position of Molly Brett's teddy bears as the guardian image of the nursery.

84 Nursery wall picture: *The Toys on Holiday* by Molly Brett, © The Medici Society Ltd., 1977.

CHAPTER 5

Nursery Books and Characters

Pictures on walls need to have a more lasting appeal, and hence more substance, than pictures in books. They do not carry the responsibility of having to illustrate a story that already has an independent existence. They have no need to reflect the changes in costume, character or incident that have developed as the story progressed. A nursery wall-picture of a little girl in a dress of the 1780s would be perfectly acceptable even today. In the wrong book it could be a ridiculous anachronism.

The most important and widespread manifestation of art for the nursery is to be found in the illustrations for children's books. The evolution of the nursery book has been a record of the development of the nursery itself. In 1850 there was little tradition on which children's book illustrators could build. The very techniques permitted to the artists were determined by the limitations of the reproduction processes of the time. Nowadays, not only is there a long history of book art, but the influence of film and television has changed the very manner of presentation of the illustrations.

Up to the middle of the nineteenth century few nursery books existed that did not have some moral purpose, and even fewer carried illustrations of quality. Illustrated contemporary fictional stories for children did not exist. Nursery books were mostly educational, and few, other than Alphabet books, were generously illustrated.

The Alphabet books themselves were an accepted part of the Victorian nursery, and were an essential tool for the instruction of every child. In the earlier books each letter of the alphabet was given a single illustration of an object whose name began with that letter, with pictures ranging

85 Animal alphabet from *Our Nursery Book*, Shaw & Co., 1895.

from the frightening realism of those for some of the Zoo Alphabets (85), to the more sophisticated coloured designs of Walter Crane and Kate Greenaway (86). The mid-1860s had brought the first colour-printed Alphabet books, and the degree of realism, combined with ingenuity in selecting themes such as 'The Alphabet of Flowers' or 'The Railway ABC', resulted in many attractive examples. The gift books of the early 1900s brought in a different style of Alphabet book in which, because of the new colour process needing a special art paper, the text and the plates were required to be separate. Themes rather than single letters were illustrated, so that one could find, for example *Peter Pan's ABC* in which each letter referred to a key word: 'B for Bath, in which Nana, so handy at scrubbing/Gave all the young Darlings a thorough good rubbing' (87). This elaboration became the forerunner of the modern, hilarious, but by no means frivolous alphabets of Dr Seuss, which tease the curiosity of the child in the best manner of modern teaching methods (88).

The ingenuity of the designer of Alphabet books was always given its severest test in the handling, or as often happened, the circumventing, of the letter 'X'. Before the invention of the xylophone or the discovery of X-rays, the illustration, all too frequently, was of 'Xmas' or the cross on 'hot-x-buns'; an expedient that even Walter Crane, in his *Absurd ABC* of 1874, was not above using. 'Xerxes' allowed the artist to indulge his ability to draw pomp and the various insignias of monarchy, usually more Arthurian than Persian in splendour. Even more esoteric, 'Xiphius', the swordfish, ranged in imaginative extravagance from a Nostradamic depiction of a flying missile in *Our Nursery Book* of 1895, to a very obvious example of

86 Kate Greenaway: 'S Sang for it', from *A Apple Pie*, George Routledge & Sons, 1886.

87 (opposite) Flora White: 'B for Bath', from *Peter Pan's ABC* by Humphrey Milford, Oxford University Press, 1914.

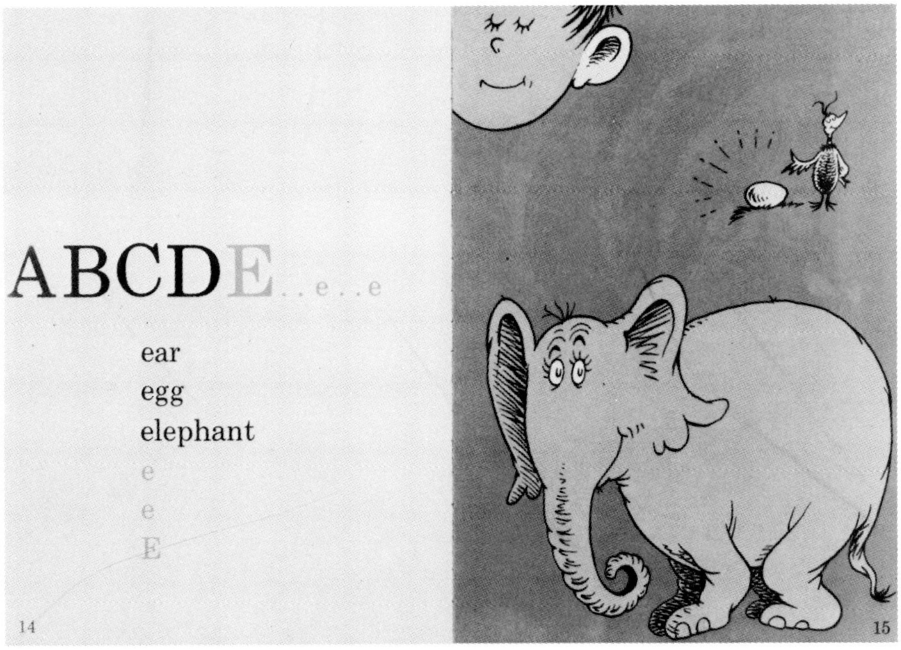

88 'ABCDE . . e . . e' from *Dr Seuss's ABC*, Random House Inc, 1963. © 1963 Dr Seuss and reprinted by permission of Random House Inc. and William Collins Sons & Co. Ltd.

taxidermal expertise in Walter Crane's *Noah's Ark ABC* of 1872. The elusive 'x' forced L.C. Healy in *John Bull's Farm Alphabet* into 'Xcellent ('. . . such is our mother, our father, our sisters and dear little brother'). *An Alphabet of Flowers* gave 'x' for 'Exotics' and showed a little girl surrounded by passion flowers and other tropical blooms. In another publication of the 1860s, *Mother's Picture Alphabet*, beside a magnificent drawing of a windswept Moses, 'x' was treated as a Roman '10' and went on to list the Ten Commandments (89). Flora White, in *Peter Pan's ABC* that was published in 1914, also played with words and showed the Lost Boys looking through their legs at the wolves as an 'Xtraordinary thing to do', while earlier, Kate Greenaway in her *A Apple Pie*, completely evaded the issue by making 'x' just one of the last few little girls who were taking a slice of the pie to bed.

Alphabet books apart, it was not until the 1840s that stories which showed a measure of understanding of what children themselves might like first appeared with Cole's *Home Treasure Series*. Writing under the name of 'Felix Summerly', Sir Henry Cole, an enlightened educationalist, inventor of the Christmas card and founder of what is now the Victoria and Albert Museum, edited and published nursery tales with illustrations commissioned from John Linnell, William Mulready and other notable artists of the day. In 1851 Ruskin's *The King of the Golden River* with its well-known frontispiece by Richard Doyle was published, but the first book written especially for children that was to achieve fame both for its story and its pictures was Thackeray's *The Rose and the Ring* of 1855 (90). The author's own illustrations for the book owed something in style to the cartoons of Gillray, a little to the work of George Cruikshank in his

89 'X is for Ten', from *The Mother's Picture Alphabet*, Partridge & Co., 1862.

less *grand guignol* moments, and even occasionally to the drawings of Flaxman or Blake. However eclectic they might have seemed, the illustrations, with their almost naïve eccentricity, have continued to this day to give a unique flavour to Thackeray's wry fairy tale.

The Rose and the Ring remained the only example in the English language of a story, specially written and illustrated for young children, to achieve 'classic' status until the publication in New York in 1862 of Clement C. Moore's *A Visit from Saint Nicholas*, which became better known, from its opening words, as *The Night Before Christmas*. F.O.C. Darley provided beautiful illustrations that still enchant with their combination of amusing caricature and sensitive evocation of the moonlit scenery of a Christmas Eve.

90 W.M. Thackeray: 'His R.H. The Prince of Crim Tartary', from *The Rose and the Ring*, 1855; pen and ink.

The Reverend Charles Kingsley's *The Water Babies* appeared the following year. This was more than a dogmatic sermon by the curate of a Hampshire village. It was an exquisitely crafted allegory, occasionally carried away by the fervour of its morality, of the redemption by symbolic baptism of a little sinner, and of the bringing to justice of Tom's oppressor Mr Grimes, Satan-like in name, behaviour and appearance.

It was the longest book so far to have been written expressly for children, and the first nursery story, apart from fairy tales, to have inspired different artists to illustrate the many editions it has received. The variety of interpretation given to these illustrations alone offers insight into the many different styles that have been used in art for the nursery.

The original edition of the book contained only two illustrations, both of them circular in form, drawn with classical simplicity by Noel Paton. In one, a perplexed Tom was shown riding on the back of a jelly-fish, a trio of Water Babies in tow. In the other, Mrs Doasyouwouldbedoneby gave instruction to Tom as he sat on her lap, his thumb in his mouth and his fellow Water Babies grouped round him like a troupe of Renaissance John the Baptists (91). Noel Paton used no colour or shading to model his figures, and the linear quality of the illustrations in, for example, the swirl

of Mrs Doasyouwouldbedoneby's hair, captured the clarity and conveyed the exact feeling of baptismal purification that the author intended.

The first fully illustrated edition was not published until 1881, when Linley Sambourne, one of the great Punch artists, provided one hundred line drawings for what purports to be the definitive edition of the book. Sambourne, as Thackeray had done in *The Rose and the Ring*, tried to establish a rapport with his young readers by using caricature and slapstick humour. Occasionally, as on the half-title, in a literal interpretation of the

91 Joseph Noel Paton: 'Mrs Doasyouwouldbedoneby', from *The Water Babies* by Charles Kingsley; pen and ink, Macmillan, 1863.

term 'a game of leapfrog', this was successful, and showed a link with Richard Doyle's work. Unfortunately though, many of the illustrations were ill-considered. Tom's encounter with the sea otter, and the migration of the eels, were depicted with frightening intensity, and even the illustration of Tom covered in prickles (while chastely clad in striped bathing drawers) was not altogether a model of serenity (92). Only rarely, as in the headpiece to the opening chapter, where a black-faced Tom gazed mournfully at the sky from the top of a chimney pot, did the artist convey the humanity that was at the heart of Kingsley's tale.

92 Linley Sambourne: 'For he was horribly ashamed of himself', from *The Water Babies*; pen and ink, Macmillan, 1881.

93 (opposite) W. Heath Robinson: 'He found Gotham where the wise men live', from *The Water Babies*, pen and ink, Constable & Co., 1915; © 1972 Estate of Mrs J.C. Robinson.

The celebrated gift book version illustrated by Warwick Goble in 1909 was also disappointing. The book itself was sumptuously produced, but the drawings had a heavy uninteresting line and the colour washes were often unimaginative. Echoes of Rackham, Dulac and Charles Robinson could be detected in the mock-orientalism of the illustrations, but all too often the simplicity looked contrived, and the almost bare settings were seen in the end to be no more than an attempt to emulate one of the tricks of photography in bleeding the edges of the picture.

The illustrations by W. Heath Robinson for the Constable edition in 1915 were far better. Although the reproduction of the colour plates was sometimes muddy and gave the babies thick dark make-up round the eyes, the black and white drawings were superb, and ranged from the clever placing of tiny figures in an infinity of white space, to the very converse of this, in which the scene was presented entirely in silhouette (93). Both in his early form as a natural larking ragamuffin and later, after his amniotic rebirth as a Water Baby, Tom was treated with the utmost sympathy by the artist.

Mabel Lucie Attwell was especially well suited to interpret *The Water Babies* for young children. Her natural style stressed the nursery elements in the book and seemed to filter out the feeling of conflict inherent in the story. Her bubbly infants were already Water Babies (94), whilst any artist who could successfully portray, as she did, Tom in tears whilst actually under water, deserves every praise.

Jessie Wilcox Smith, in her version for Dodd Meade's of New York in 1916, showed the greatest sympathy and understanding of the actual role of the characters. Every nursery child would recognize the nanny figure of Mrs Doasyouwouldbedoneby, who was drawn as a chuckling, warm, new-bready person, so much more inviting than Noel Paton's remote goddess. As with all her drawings, the figures were modelled from life, with Tom as a black-haired child with an endearing quiff and perfect tiny features, guaranteed to win the heart of any mother (C15).

Both Katherine Cameron in 1908, with her Glasgow School of Art background, and Alice B. Woodward in 1909, illustrated *The Water Babies* in the Art Nouveau manner. It was a style that was admirably suited to capturing the ripple and swirl of the water and the fanciful world under the sea. But perhaps the loveliest illustrations done in this way were those by Ann Anderson in 1924 when Art Nouveau, as a movement, was all but

C16 'Little Boy Blue' from *Mother Goose's Nursery Rhymes*, McLoughlin Bros., New York, *c.* 1880.

94 Mabel Lucie Attwell: end paper for *The Water Babies*; pen and ink, Raphael Tuck & Sons Ltd., 1915. © Lucie Attwell Ltd.

95 Ann Anderson: 'Oh you beautiful creature', from *The Water Babies*; pencil and watercolour, T.C. & E.C. Jack Ltd., 1924.

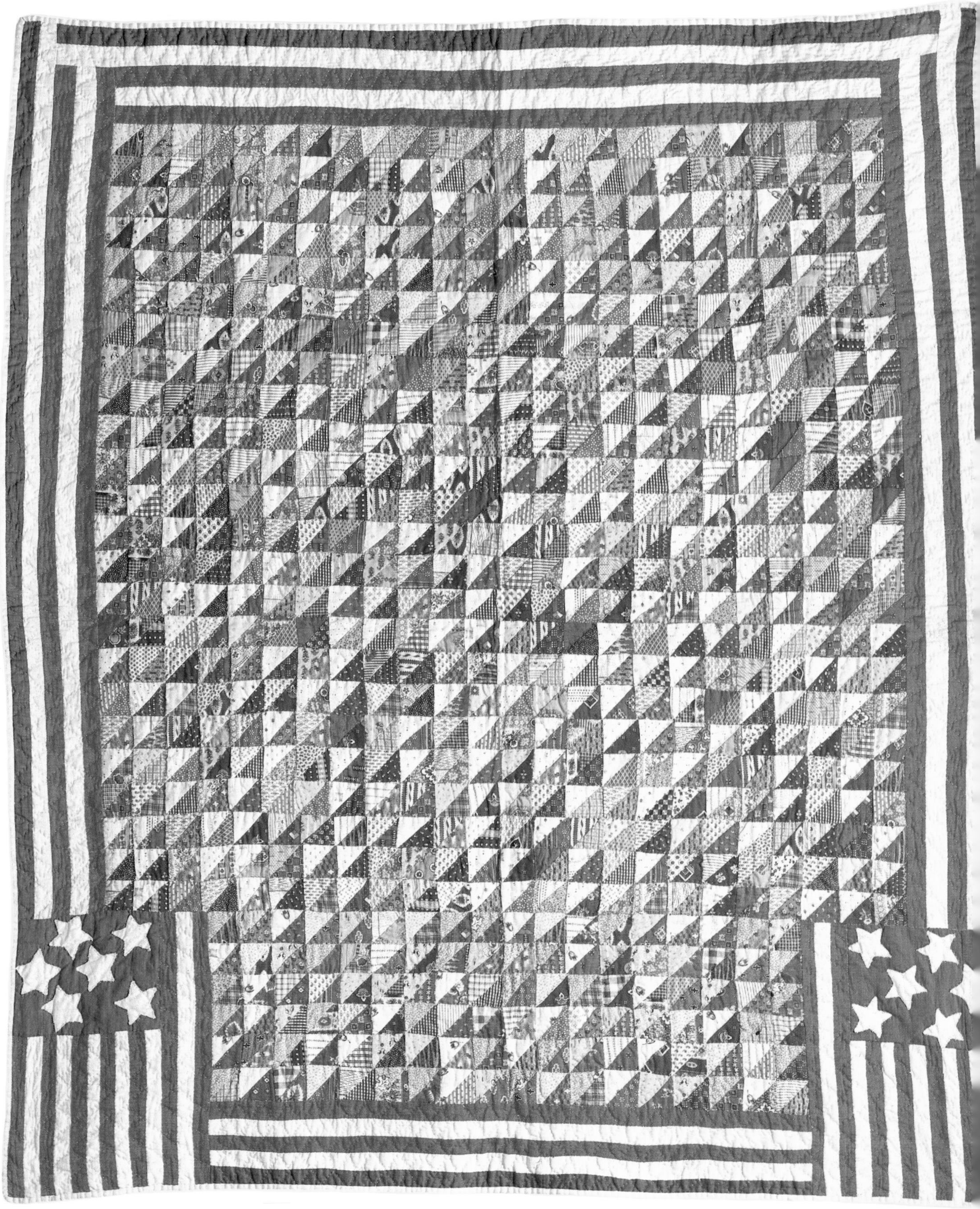

extinct. Her careful study of the child's anatomy – a baby really would reach up to a dragonfly in the way that Tom is made to do – was not made an end, in the way that Jessie Wilcox Smith's had been, but a basis for imaginative elaboration. These illustrations had a fantasy and inventiveness that captured, as no others have done, the sense of grace and the dreamlike quality of Charles Kingsley's story (95).

Such a variety of illustration could only have been produced for a book whose story provided a framework for imagination and inventiveness. Books like these become the classics of the nursery. They occur rarely, even in countries with a flourishing literary tradition. The American contribution in the nineteenth century to this distinguished company, with *A Night Before Christmas*, *Yankee Doodle*, *Uncle Remus* and, in a sense, *Uncle Tom's Cabin*, was considerable and significant.

During the first half of the nineteenth century most of the books published in the United States were reprints of British editions. Nevertheless, a few original illustrated books for children appeared surprisingly early. The McLoughlin Brothers of New York, for example, had published *The History of Little Goody Two Shoes* with illustrations by John Absolom as early as 1855. The picture books for which they became famous (their equivalent of the British 'Toy Books') first appeared in the 1860s, their pictorial covers, often with elaborate ornamentation in reds, yellows, greens and gold, gave an impression of fairground garishness and made them instantly recognizable. For half a century 'McLoughlins' were the most popular children's books in the United States. There were McLoughlin farmyard books, counting books and shaped books, in imitation of the ones by Dean's and Nelson's in Great Britain. McLoughlin's had their versions of the standard fairy tales and nursery rhymes with chromolithograph plates and black and white illustrations, many by the talented J.H. Howard (C16), (96). They varied in quality, from the utmost sensitivity to an earthy vulgarity that would have debarred them from many nurseries on both sides of the Atlantic but, in general, they offered well-printed texts and attractive illustrations at very modest prices.

In the United States, as in Great Britain, the reading class was the middle class, and it was towards this complacent, servant-owning society that *Uncle Tom's Cabin*, which was written in 1850–1 as a serial for a magazine, was directed. However patronizing the manner, here, for the first time, the slave was treated as a sentient human being. To speak with disapproval of 'Uncle Tomism' is to overlook the fact that in 1850 there was nothing else. Three years later a version for young children was published with the text in unbelievably mawkish verse and with appropriately sentimental illustrations by an unnamed artist. Couplets such as 'Dry the eyes for holy Eva,/With the blessed angels leave her', seem maudlin to modern so-called sophistication but, in its day, a text such as this was regarded as an acceptable level of communication to a nursery

C17 Crib quilt, 1862. Pieced cotton, 43½ in. × 36 in. Private collection, USA. Photograph: American Hurrah Antiques, New York.

96 'Little Mary had a Lamb' from *Mother Goose's Nursery Rhymes*, McLoughlin Bros., New York, *c.* 1880.

When Mary missed her little lamb,
She raised a dreadful wail;
Just then a fireman pulled it out,
And saved it by the tail.

child of a situation that confronted the whole nation.

After the Civil War, attitudes towards differences of colour tended to become rationalized as class distinction. In *Holiday Songs* that L. J. Bridgman illustrated in 1901, amid rousing songs for Washington's Birthday and for Thanksgiving, an illustration for 'The Bowing Game', with white and black children playing together, showed an evident status difference between them, in both dress and bearing. As the status rose, so patronizing sentimentality developed towards the black servant in children's literature. 'The Little Teacher', in which a white child was shown teaching the aged family retainer his letters, was only one example of what was really a sincere attempt to overlay years of conditioning to a slave-owning society with a veneer of good manners.

Uncle Remus was, perhaps, outside such a critique, for the tales that Joel Chandler Harris wrote between 1880 and 1908 were really fables, much in the manner of Aesop's, set against a background of the Deep South. Harris's choice of A.B. Frost as an illustrator, after his disappointment with the original illustrations by Moser and Church, was a wise one. Frost's drawings conveyed, with remarkable intensity, the feel of the heat and dustiness of the South (97). He left extensive areas of the paper untouched in order to underline the contrast between the heavy sunlight and deep shadows, and his use of a scrabbled dotted line to depict the road, interspersed with more flexible strokes to suggest wild grass, now bring to mind the early work of his contemporary Arthur Rackham.

97 A.B. Frost: ''Mawnin'' from *Uncle Remus* by Joel Chandler Harris, D. Appleton and Co., New York, 1881.

98 Sir John Tenniel: 'In another moment Alice was through the glass', from *Through the Looking Glass* by Lewis Carroll, Macmillan, 1871.

Frost's illustrations are as much a part of the *Uncle Remus* stories as are Tenniel's of *Alice*. In 1865, two years after the publication of *The Water Babies*, the seven-year-old Alice was feeling sleepy as she sat by her sister on the bank. 'What', she thought pertinently, 'is the use of a book without pictures?' The Alice we visualize is, of course, Tenniel's as much as Lewis Carroll's. Nowhere in the book is Alice described in words and yet, with Tenniel's illustrations, every fragment of the story is made to relate to the little girl he has pictured. We immediately think of the pinafore, the slippers and the long blond hair with the Alice-band.

The ultimate mark of success of a storybook character is for an article of clothing to be named after it. There have been the Peter Pan collar; the Buster Suit, after R.F. Outcault's American tearaway; the Rupert Bear

99 (opposite) Arthur Rackham: 'Advice from a Caterpillar', from *Alice's Adventures Underground*, pen, ink and watercolour, Heinemann, 1907.

trousers; the Noddy Hat and, perhaps, the Kate Greenaway dress and the Dolly Varden bonnet. The Alice-band belongs to this select company. The irony is that the Alice in Wonderland of Tenniel's illustrations never wore an Alice-band. She was not even Alice Liddell, the dark-haired little girl for whom the book was written, but was one of Lewis Carroll's photographed subjects, Mary Hilton Badcock. Tenniel drew her accurately: a bad-tempered-looking little girl, younger, shorter and plumper than the Alice that Carroll himself drew in *Alice's Adventures Underground*, as the original manuscript was called. In Carroll's photograph Mary Badcock is, indeed, wearing the famous Alice-band, but, in the book as published, Alice's hair is ribbonless and swept back tightly from the forehead. Only when she went through the Looking Glass was she wearing the famous ribbon; with the bow, let all ambitious mothers note, on the left (98).

In the seven years that separated *Wonderland* from *Through the Looking Glass*, Alice had neither aged nor grown. She had changed her plain white stockings for the more famous ones with Dutch stripes but, despite the addition of a frilly border to her pinafore, her dress was the same. Consequently, it took great courage on the part of Arthur Rackham in 1909 to attempt to usurp Tenniel and present Alice with her hair held back by grips, wearing black stockings, with lace-up shoes rather than slippers, and with smocking at the waist rather than apron strings (99).

Although he was a far greater illustrator than Tenniel, and his finished pictures for *Alice in Wonderland* more skilfully executed, Rackham's Alice never displaced the archetypal image that Tenniel had created. It is for the glory of the completed pictures that one remembers Rackham's illustrations; the exquisite summer afternoons of the Mad Hatter's Tea Party; the Queen of Hearts, portly as a Toby jug, raging at the Barrow-boy Jack of Hearts; or the magnificent picture of Alice with the Nestorian caterpillar as the age-old possessor of total wisdom.

Out of approximately a hundred artists who have illustrated Alice (and they include the American Peter Newell, more famous for his trick books than for his illustrations of classics; Willy Pogany, who made his Alice a low-waisted tomboy of the 'twenties, in short socks and strap-over patent leather shoes; and Salvador Dali, for whom the surrealism of the stories ideally suited his particular genius) not one has been able to impose his image on the book and displace Tenniel's. Despite the many different forms in which Alice has been introduced to the nursery – from the tea service which Doulton produced in 1906, to the curtain fabric and tiles which the great architect C.F.A. Voysey designed as a reinterpretation of Tenniel's own drawings in terms of the technique and fashions of the 'thirties – it is always to Tenniel's original illustrations that one turns for the definitive Alice.

In the same year that *Alice in Wonderland* was published in Britain,

Arthur Rackham 07

there appeared in the United States a much slimmer volume containing one single poem, *Yankee Doodle*, that was to become America's greatest contribution to nursery song. It was illustrated by F.O.C. Darley in a style very different from the one he had used for *A Visit from Saint Nicholas*. Here, with a brilliant feeling for caricature, and the same disrespect for rank or dignity as a Phiz, he portrayed Yankee Doodle as a stubble-haired yokel, and his father as a tipsy asinine squire, hopelessly incompetent with the apparatus of war. It was a picture that King George III had found to his cost to be woefully inaccurate. One of the illustrations, that of the little drummer boy (100), deserves immortality, for it was not surpassed even by the great Howard Pyle in his illustrations for the poem a quarter of a century later.

Yankee Doodle provided America with its first images of patriotism; a sentiment that was to remain unfed until the bitterness that led to the tragedy of the Civil War involved many more people in the concept of 'My Country'. It entered the nursery, not only in the form of picture books and clothes for dressing up like daddy, but in such unlikely ways as songs of homage to the veterans (101) and a superb example of that very typical American folk art, the patchwork crib quilt with its six stars at each corner representing the original states of the Confederacy (C17).

Nursery illustration in Britain and America, however different in theme and style, was united in 1895 by the Golliwogg. In the beginning there was only one Golliwogg, with a capital 'G'. Dressed in a short blue jacket, red trousers and a floppy bow-tie, he was unique, male and the creation of Florence K. Upton (102). The Uptons, although British, had lived in the United States for a number of years. On the death of her father, Florence returned to Britain with her mother, Bertha Upton, to stay with relatives. Here her first book about Golliwogg, *The Adventures of Two Dutch Dolls*, was written by Bertha and illustrated by Florence with coloured drawings based on the dolls that the Upton girls had owned as children.

100 F.O.C. Darley: 'Yankee Doodle', pen and ink, Trent, Filmer & Co., New York, 1865.

The immediate success of the book was not, as had originally been intended, because of the dolls but because of Golliwogg. The Uptons showed an initial hesitation about how the character should be developed. Golliwogg's first entry was described by Bertha as: 'Then all look round, as well they may,/To see a horrid sight,/The blackest gnome stands there alone,/They scatter all in fright.' The drawings, too, had something repellent about them, for Golliwogg was always made huge and menacing by the side of the slender Dutch dolls. He was always polite, but never smiled, so that one was uncertain whether his next act would be friendly or not. Perhaps this was a deliberate and clever way of maintaining tension and promoting greater joy when its resolution came.

The Uptons quickly realized Golliwogg's potential as a kind and compassionate friend within the nursery, and the twelve sequels they wrote at yearly intervals, with adventures in places as various as an airship, a circus

101 L.J. Bridgman: 'Soldiers True' from *Holiday Songs* by Emilie Poulson, Milton Bradley Co., Springfield, Massachusetts, 1901.

or the African jungle, established the personality of Golliwogg as a lovable one, and confirmed the popularity of their creation.

Neither Florence Upton nor her publishers could have foreseen the extent to which Golliwogg was to appeal to children throughout the world, and no attempt was made to take out a copyright on either the name or the image of 'Golly', an abbreviation that the Uptons themselves introduced. For many years every child owned one of the soft rag dolls, and the Golliwogg image was to be found on china, pottery figurines and greetings cards, as well as on the label of Robertson's jams and the cover of

C18 (opposite above) 'Jack and the Beanstalk', from *Our Nurse's Picture Book*, George Routledge & Sons, London and New York, 1870. Chromolithograph plate by Kronheim & Co.

C19 (opposite below) Baby carriage, New England, *c.* 1880. Collection Tasha Tudor.

C20 (overleaf) Margaret W. Tarrant: *All Things Bright and Beautiful*, nursery picture, 1925, The Medici Society Ltd., London.

Debussy's *Children's Corner Suite*. Nowadays, for racial reasons, the Golliwogg, as a doll, is no longer made, but in the years of his existence he has been one of the best loved inhabitants of the nursery and has brought immeasurable pleasure to generations of children.

102 Florence K. Upton: 'They scatter in their fright ...', from *The Adventures of Two Dutch Dolls* by Bertha Upton, Longmans, Green & Co., 1895.

Even more than Golly, however, the one character who has reigned unchallenged in the nursery has been the Teddy Bear. Theodore Roosevelt's act of magnanimity towards the two orphaned bear cubs, that earned him immortality, was brought to the nursery in 1906, first as a newspaper series written by Seymour Eaton, and then as a book compiled of their adventures with illustrations by Floyd Campbell. The bears, Teddy B. (for 'Boy') and Teddy G. (for 'Girl'), were portrayed, as Louis Wain had his cats, keeping their animal appearance, but dressed up in various costumes and allowed human expressions. The adventures took place entirely in America and the books were not published in Great Britain. Only when, as a result of the huge success of the books, the familiar 'Teddy' of the nursery, with its warm-coloured glass eyes and rough golden plush, was manufactured, did this universal comforter and children's confidant cross the Atlantic to become so completely the favourite pet that his American origins are all but forgotten, and a time when there were no Teddies seems inconceivable (57).

ALL THINGS BRIGHT AND BEAUTIF
ALL THINGS WISE & WONDERFU

CREATURES GREAT AND SMALL
Margaret W Tarrant
LORD GOD MADE THEM ALL

The WHITE BINDWEED Fairy

CHAPTER 6

The Fairies

C21 Cicely Barker: 'The White Bindweed Fairy' from *Cicely Barker's Flower Fairy Picture Book*, Blackie & Sons Ltd., 1955.

If the most powerful single image presented to children in the nursery has been the Teddy Bear, the ones that have provided the greatest stimuli to the child's imagination have come from Fairyland. In all shapes and forms fairies have been made to explain the inexplicable, used as a vehicle for the fantastic and become a mechanism whereby dreams and nightmares have been allowed to come true.

Fairies watched over cradles long before nurseries began. They have been looked upon as both benign and malevolent, either guarding the baby from harm, or waiting for an opportunity to change the infant for one of their own, according to the taste of the time. Within the nursery they belong to certain accepted classifications. In increasing order of benevolence towards little children these have been: Gnomes, who are individual, humanoid and grotesque; Hobgoblins, who are spiky and grey, with staring eyes and bald heads, threatening the selfish and spiteful with pinches and nips; Elves, who are greenish and good when young but who, when older, become gnome-like and are not very nice to know; Brownies, who come in hordes and, as Palmer Cox demonstrated, are the workers of the hive, those unseen nocturnal helpers of Beatrix Potter's *The Tailor of Gloucester* and Andersen's *The Little Shoemakers*; and Pixies, who are very light in weight, have a sense of humour but are rather useless, especially in their pubescent form as Sprites, and are best confined to the pages of children's comics.

Fairies proper, who gave their name to the whole order, are the most variable, both in size and behaviour. They have been pictured in many forms and shapes, from the gibbering menace of Richard Dadd's manikins, to the substantial but insipid nudes of Victorian salon painters, with Edmund Dulac's 'Ariel' and W. Heath Robinson's 'Puck' coming somewhere in between. They vary from the thistledown lightness of Tinker Bell to Jessie M. King's slender maidens, each as beautiful and remote as a young mother passing through the nursery on her way to a ball (103). In their adult form they can vary, in both age and beauty, from the Christmas-tree-type of fairy, tutued and wand-bearing, to the old wizened, nanny-like creatures typified by the Fairy Carabosse of *The Sleeping Beauty* or the fairy godmother in *Cinderella*. The older they get the more touchy they become, and the more readily they use their powers for vengeful acts after some, often imagined, slight.

103 Jessie M. King: 'The Magic Garret', from *Littledom Castle and Other Tales* by Mrs M.H. Spielmann, Routledge, 1903.

104 Richard Doyle: 'Cruel Elves', from *In Fairyland*, Longmans, Green, Reader & Dyer, 1870.

Giving form to the fairies has always tested the inventive powers of illustrators. For a number of years Victorian fairies, in books and, more particularly, at Royal Academy exhibitions, were depicted as Iolanthes or Giselles in three-quarter-length ballet dresses with wings sprouting from their shoulders. Occasionally, when they made a sudden appearance before a mortal, they would be depicted as pagan equivalents of the Angel in a Renaissance painting of the Annunciation, with the fairy wand, in various forms, replacing the proferred lily (C18).

It was Richard Doyle, in his *In Fairyland*, who first showed the whole range of the fairy kingdom. Doyle had been a Punch artist and was the designer of the famous cover that most people bring to mind when they think of that magazine. *In Fairyland*, which was published in 1870, beautifully printed in colour by Edmund Evans was, like Wagner's 'Ring', assembled in reverse order. The pictures were drawn by Doyle first, and the text, a poem by William Allingham, written afterwards. Doyle's fairies were not the exquisite dancers of Barrie's *Peter Pan*, but were the grotesque caricatures of human freaks that belonged to the Gothic re-creations of Dadd and Fuseli (104). They were ruled by the Elf King, whose long hair and three strands of moustachios were born by a retinue of his unruly subjects, with pet snails, doormice and butterflies in tow. This world, run wild, produced the effete monsters of Beardsley and his followers. Tamed, however, it led to the Brownies: a manic crowd of amorphous jelly-babies, devised by the American illustrator Palmer Cox (105).

105 Palmer Cox: 'The Brownies on Skates', from *The Brownies, their Book*, The Century Company, New York, 1887.

The Brownies first appeared in the magazine *Saint Nicholas*, the drawings laid out in sequence, very much like the forerunners of children's comics. Only later, in 1887, when they were established favourites, did the adventures of the Brownies appear in book form. Brueghel-like assemblages of little creatures were common in children's book illustration of the mid-nineteenth century, and Cruikshank's and Thomas Nast's hobgoblins, as well as Richard Doyle's processions of fairy folk were all examples of this gregariousness. In their attempts to be of service, the Brownies tackled problems of a human scale by the application of a great number of tiny units of energy. Compelled to help by their genetic make-up, their over-eagerness invariably landed them in trouble. Some of the Brownies were given individual characteristics and, in many of the stories, it was possible to pick out one's favourites: possibly the Scottish Brownie with the tam; the Policeman Brownie, the Black Brownie twins or the monacled and top-hatted Brownie Toff.

The Brownies skated, tobogganed, rode penny-farthings and went to the circus, the fair and the zoo, always at night when everybody was asleep. Whatever pranks they got up to, by daybreak everything was tidy, broken things were mended, and wherever there had been need they left plenty.

In one of the stories the Brownies stole into a pawnshop to borrow skates. As the rhyming text described it: 'The place is filled with various things,/From baby carts to banjo strings.' One of the Brownies was shown sitting in a baby carriage, the design of which and, indeed, the very use in the tale of the term 'Baby cart', helped to place the drawing in the context of its time (105).

Up to 1875 it was illegal, in both Britain and the United States, to use a four-wheeled vehicle on the footpath, and so all baby carriages had either two or three wheels. Very young babies were given their airing carried in the arms of their mothers or nurses, swathed in long embroidered or lace draperies designed to show off the infant. The early baby carriages, in the 1850s, were padded three-wheeled vehicles of a sweeping, almost Art Nouveau design (106) that were intended for the older child, as was the slightly later carriage and pair with its galloping horses and coachman's whip (107). Much simpler than this was the 'Mail cart': a two-wheeled vehicle made of wood, which was stable when parked but very uncomfortable (108). Like the three-wheeler it was designed only for sitting up in. The comfort of the younger baby was taken into account only around 1870 with the idea of mounting the baby's bassinet on wheels. This, it was argued, was no more than a convenient way of moving a cradle from place to place and was in no way an infringement of the laws about road vehicles. The four-wheeled baby carriage had arrived and, as soon as the bassinet, hitherto confined to the nursery itself, was subjected to the public gaze, fashion and design and the associated snobberies became of importance.

The British climate required a baby carriage with solid sides, but in the United States it was possible to use a more open vehicle, like the baby cart made in the 1880s for the Tudor family in New England (C19). For town dwellers concerned about status, fancy bodywork was imported from France, Sweden and even Africa, where the choice of exotic woods was greater. The baby carriage became a wheeled nest of criss-cross basketry, with the randing woven into ovals, diamonds and quatrefoils. Lined with satin and bearing either a dainty parasol or a more substantial collapsible hood, it was ultimately suspended on coach springs and so protected the infant from upset by the cobblestones below or the inclement weather above (109).

106 Baby carriage: the Parker model, 1850. Collection of Jack Hampshire Baby Carriage Museum, Kent.

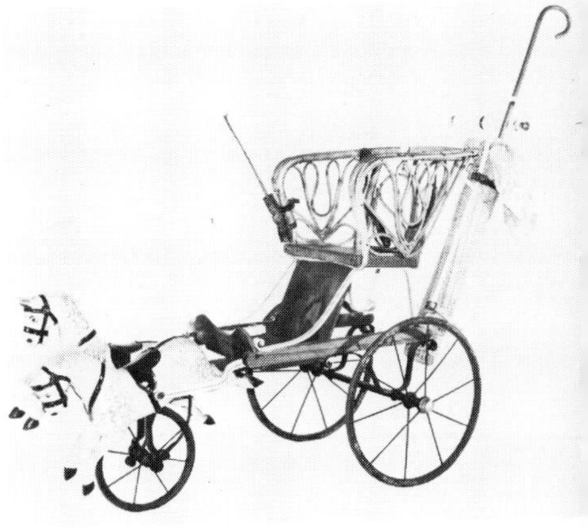

107 Baby carriage: 'Carriage and Pair', 1870. Collection of Jack Hampshire.

108 Baby carriage: back-to-back Mailcart, 1880. Collection of Jack Hampshire.

109 Baby carriage: four-wheeled baby carriage with reeded cane sides, 1890. Collection of Jack Hampshire.

By 1900 the pram had finally begun to evolve as the four-wheeled vehicle we recognize today, its distinction shown more by the quality of its workmanship and simplicity of line than by the flamboyant eccentricities of former years.

It would seem, therefore, that the four-wheeled baby carriage in which the Brownie was sitting must have been built after 1875 and before 1887 when Palmer Cox drew it. From the styling it appears to have been derived from the Parker model of 1850 and, despite its somewhat forlorn appearance, the parasol points to its having been designed for more halcyon days than when the Brownies found it in the pawnshop one frosty night.

Unlike the Brownies, winged fairies did not need baby carriages to transport their young. Rose Fyleman, whose poems helped to determine the form of fairies for the twentieth century, suggested that broomsticks, similar to those of witches, were their standard mode of transport, although the narrator in one of her verses claimed to have seen the Fairy Queen riding on a bus in Oxford Street. The wings, it would seem, were used only for hovering over flowers or cradles. Whether the Fyleman poems were responsible, or whether the illustrators were reacting against the malevolent streak in fairies that had been noticeable for so long, it was the alate nymph that was to become the dominant species in the fairy world between the two world wars. This, as will be seen, was the prototype of all the mutations, from Walt Disney's interpretation of Tinker Bell to the Tooth Fairy, that have appeared since.

After World War I, Mabel Lucie Attwell's 'Kiddiwinks' still lisped their way through nurseries in their DD fitting shoes as if nothing had changed. The fairies and mermaids of Ann Anderson still floated through the clouds and waves that folded round them protectively. The artists of this reverie were as popular as ever, with Margaret Tarrant as perhaps the principal recorder of those dancing-class fairies, made to epitomize the cleanest, prettiest and most well-behaved little girls imaginable. If nowadays one is disturbed by the bland sentimentality of some of Margaret Tarrant's work it should be remembered that she was a sincerely devout person and that her fairy pictures, as well as the many beautiful religious ones that she painted in a Pre-Raphaelite manner, were expressions of an inner joy she wished to share (C20). Every one of her pictures was sensitively drawn and painted. The look of wonder on the faces of the children in 'Do you believe in Fairies?', and the clever play of light from the setting sun on the fairies themselves, were admirably caught and very difficult to execute (83). Her art was far greater, both technically and imaginatively than the stereotyped bible figures that were to be found in so many nursery pictures, and far more worthy of a place on the nursery wall.

Margaret Tarrant was only one of several artists of the period who brought fresh insight into how fairies really looked. The new fairies, for the most part, were children rather than sprites or benevolent witches, and offered an immediate invitation to the little readers to identify themselves with the image. Many of the children's annuals between the wars contained fairy illustrations by artists who worked in this manner. Molly Brett, Cicely Barker, Ann Anderson, Hilda T. Miller, Florence Anderson and Ida Rentoul Outhwaite in Australia all shared this new conception of fairies that Rose Fyleman had written about in her poems (110). No issue of *The Joy Book*, *The Chummy Book* or *Playbox Annual* in the 'twenties was complete without its fairy pictures. Cicely Barker's 'Flower Fairies' pictures, so beautifully finished that the surfaces seemed to have had their faces powdered, began to appear in nurseries (C21). Hilda T. Miller illustrated an edition of Rose Fyleman's poems themselves, in a style not unlike that of the early Dulac, with great charm and merit, and Florence Anderson's illustrations for Lady Margaret Saville's *The Dream Pedlar* confirmed how very much a school had arisen amongst these, almost invariably, lady illustrators.

With few exceptions the fairy cult by-passed the United States, as if the glades of Vermont lacked the age-old mysteries of the New Forest. One book, *The Catskill Fairies* by Virginia Johnson, with a number of woodcuts by Alfred Fredericks depicting fairies in the Victorian manner as diminutive Taglionis, was published in New York in 1876. Much later, in 1930, Harrison Cady illustrated Sherman Ripley's *The Raggedies in Fairyland* and portrayed the fairies as winged ephemera of vapid insignificance, with antennae and pointed ears and chins (111). Indigenous fairies in the United States were, however, little in evidence until they appeared in their most recent manifestations as the various avatars of the Tooth Fairy. Although its final delineament, and indeed sex, has yet to be decided – it has appeared both winged and wingless; wand-bearing and wandless; young as the All-American girl and old as Whistler's mother – it has, since its arrival in America in the late 1940s, become an enthusiastically welcomed personification of those nameless British fairies who used to creep

110 Molly Brett: 'The Three Blackie Beetles' from *Wonder Book*, Ward Lock & Co., 1925.

C22 Nursery fabric. Pixie O'Harris: 'The Fairy who wouldn't Fly', printed cotton, manufactured by A.E. Hoad & Co. Pty. Ltd., Sydney, 1969; © Pixie O'Harris, 1976.

under pillows or wade through saucers of salt water to exchange newly shed teeth for a halfpenny. One can buy in the United States nowadays a miniature pillow, sometimes tooth-shaped, with a pocket large enough to take both a shed tooth and the dollar bill expected in exchange. Such is the munificence of fairies in these times of inflation.

111 Harrison Cady: 'You mustn't do that ...' from *The Raggedies in Fairyland* by Sherman Ripley, 1930.

One of the most important of the fairy illustrators was the Australian, Ida Rentoul Outhwaite. In her very early work she had pictured Australian themes with remarkable sensitivity. The pen and ink illustrations she did in 1910 for *Bush Songs of Australia* had a range of textures as various as the crispness of the straw of a hat and the stubbliness of the coat of a kangaroo (112). However, the success of her first fairy book *Elves and*

Fairies in 1916 brought her London exhibitions and a British publisher, and put an end to the Australian references that had given her work such distinction. In the fairy watercolours that made her famous, set against silhouetted and gnarled trees that echoed Rackham's, were to be found the same lightly clad nymphets with permanent waves who inhabited the British fairy world (113).

C23 Helen Stratton: 'A Young Princess Held out her Hand to him', from *Andersen's Fairy Tales*, John F. Shaw & Co., London, 1896. Chromolithograph plate.

The one group of fairy characters who were both original and Australian in concept was May Gibbs's 'Gumnut Babies'. Led by 'Snugglepot' and 'Cuddlepie', the Gumnuts were as lovable and mischievous a band of scallywags as Palmer Cox's Brownies. May Gibbs wanted her work to teach Australian children the joys of their local countryside with its unique vegetation and animal life. Within a slightly Art Nouveau idiom she found expression for the shapes and colours of the delicate yellow and orange flowers of the eucalyptus tree set against the grey-green of its leaves.

112 Ida Rentoul Outhwaite: 'Hop-and-Go-One', from *Bush Songs of Australia for Young and Old*, words by Annie R. Rentoul, George Robertson & Co., Melbourne, 1910.

113 Ida Rentoul Outhwaite: 'The Queen of the Butterflies', from *Elves and Fairies* by Annie R. Rentoul, The Lothian Book Publishing Co., Melbourne & Sydney, 1916.

114 Nursery fabric: 'The Gumnuts' by May Gibbs, printed cotton, Turnbull & Stockdale, 1929.

The Gumnut stories, with their whimsical illustrations, were successful in both Britain and Australia. Sequels and new editions followed, with the ultimate accolade in 1925 of the Gumnuts' being made the subject of a comic strip in a Sydney newspaper, and of the characters' being reproduced on children's handkerchiefs and fabric shortly afterwards (114).

Ida Rentoul Outhwaite never had the commitment to the Australian scene that May Gibbs showed, but her significance lay in the fact that, together with her compatriot Pixie O'Harris, she helped to introduce the very northern concept of the fairy into a new continent.

The fairy presence in Australia has been preserved in the books written and illustrated by Pixie O'Harris (115). Her colours, possibly because of the brightness of her surroundings, are stronger and more exciting than those of any other illustrator of the fairies. She has been faithful to her Australian background, mingling elves with the Australian animals in, for example, the nursery fabric she has designed and, more significantly, in the delightful mural decorations she did for the wards of the Royal Alexandra Children's Hospital in New South Wales (C22), (116).

In Pixie O'Harris the fairies have possibly found their last and most loyal protector. Elsewhere, weakened by the arrival of the American

115 (left) Pixie O'Harris: 'The Dance of the Sea Bubble' from *Pearl Pinkie and Sea Greenie*, Angus & Robertson, 1935; © Pixie O'Harris, 1935.

116 (above) Pixie O'Harris: mural for the Royal Alexandra Children's Hospital, New South Wales, *c.* 1972.

school of realist illustrators, they were to be blown away as so much chaff by World War II. Indeed, the fairy bands were scarcely able to withstand an earlier invasion by a small bear with the unlikely name of Pooh, who, in the mid-'twenties, stomped into the hearts of English-speaking children everywhere.

CHAPTER 7

The Impact of Colour Printing

A society which looked upon children's books as an aid to education rather than as a means of entertainment, tended to be more interested in words than in pictures. Only after the middle of the eighteenth century did illustrations come to be used for decoration rather than to explain a precept. By the 1860s, the technique of lithography and the art of engraving on wood and metal had brought black and white illustration to a high level of fidelity to an artist's intentions. No satisfactory method of colour printing, though, had yet been found, and nothing quite matched the quality of the painstakingly hand-coloured lithographed plates.

As far back as the 1830s attempts had been made, notably by George Baxter, to reproduce paintings using oil colours in multiple superimposed printings from engraved blocks, with results that were extraordinarily faithful to the original pictures. A simplified and less expensive adaptation of this was used by Thomas Nelson's to illustrate their 'Oil Coloured Picture Books' of the 1860s. The colours of the large full-page illustrations were made even more vibrant by being printed against near-black backgrounds. The vivid pictures for once overshadowed in importance the contrived rhymes and clotted syntax of verses, so typical of the time, that included such labyrinthine convolutions as 'Away they went, those pretty babes/Rejoicing at that tide/Rejoicing with merry mind/They should in cock-horse ride'.

Two systems - chromolithography, which used oil-based colours printed from a flat surface; and colour printing from engraved woodblocks - offered the most promise for book work. The process of chromolithography was originally developed in Germany, mainly because the best lithographic stone came from Bavaria. This explains the not infrequent use of Gothic lettering for the titles of some of the coloured pictures in books in English. For many years British publishers sent to the Continent for their colour printing, although some of the German companies like Kronheim's and Nister's had branches in Great Britain. Chromolithographs, when they were well done, could be very attractive, and a reproduction of the work of E.V. Boyle or Helen Stratton, for example, could achieve a subtlety and richness of colour that no other method of printing has been able to match (C23).

Coloured engravings had been used to illustrate the first of the 'Toy books' – 'toy' in the sense of 'trifle' – that Dean and Son's had produced in the 1850s. This company had also been the first to woo their customers with the use of emotive names for their publications, beginning, in 1845, with a series of teaching books which they called the 'Grandpa Easy' books. They named the new nursery Toy books the 'Mama Lovechild' series. Each subsequent publisher who entered this increasingly lucrative market tried to invent a title that would add a similar homely touch, so that there appeared books from 'Aunt Affable' and 'Aunt Louisa' and, in the United States, 'Uncle Frank' and 'Uncle Buncle'.

New standards of quality in colour engraving were achieved by Edmund Evans in the 1860s. The accuracy of his blocks, the care he gave to their superimposition, and the subtlety of his inks, allowed him to reproduce, with great sensitivity, the delicacy and translucency of watercolours. Evans was an independent printer who hired out his services to interested publishers, and it was his association with the firms of Routledge and F. Warne that finally established the nursery picture book in Britain and America.

In 1865 Evans invited the young Walter Crane who, at twenty, already had four years' professional experience as an illustrator, to design Toy books for him, each consisting of a single tale illustrated in colour and costing sixpence. These slim books, alphabet books, nursery rhymes and fairy tales, were published by Routledge's as their 'Aunt Mavor' series. They were more sophisticated, in both lay-out and illustration, than anything that had been attempted before. Stories and pictures that sought to moralize, or to depict anything that might frighten children, were totally unacceptable to Crane and Evans. Their aim was to make the most attractive, the best illustrated and the most faithfully printed nursery books ever produced. They succeeded so well that pirated, as well as genuine examples appeared in the United States as early as 1870, and groups of the stories in several different combinations have remained in print ever since.

In 1876 Walter Crane began to illustrate more ambitious and more expensive nursery books for Evans, of which the first, *The Baby's Opera*, the most famous of all Crane's books, was a collection of nursery rhymes

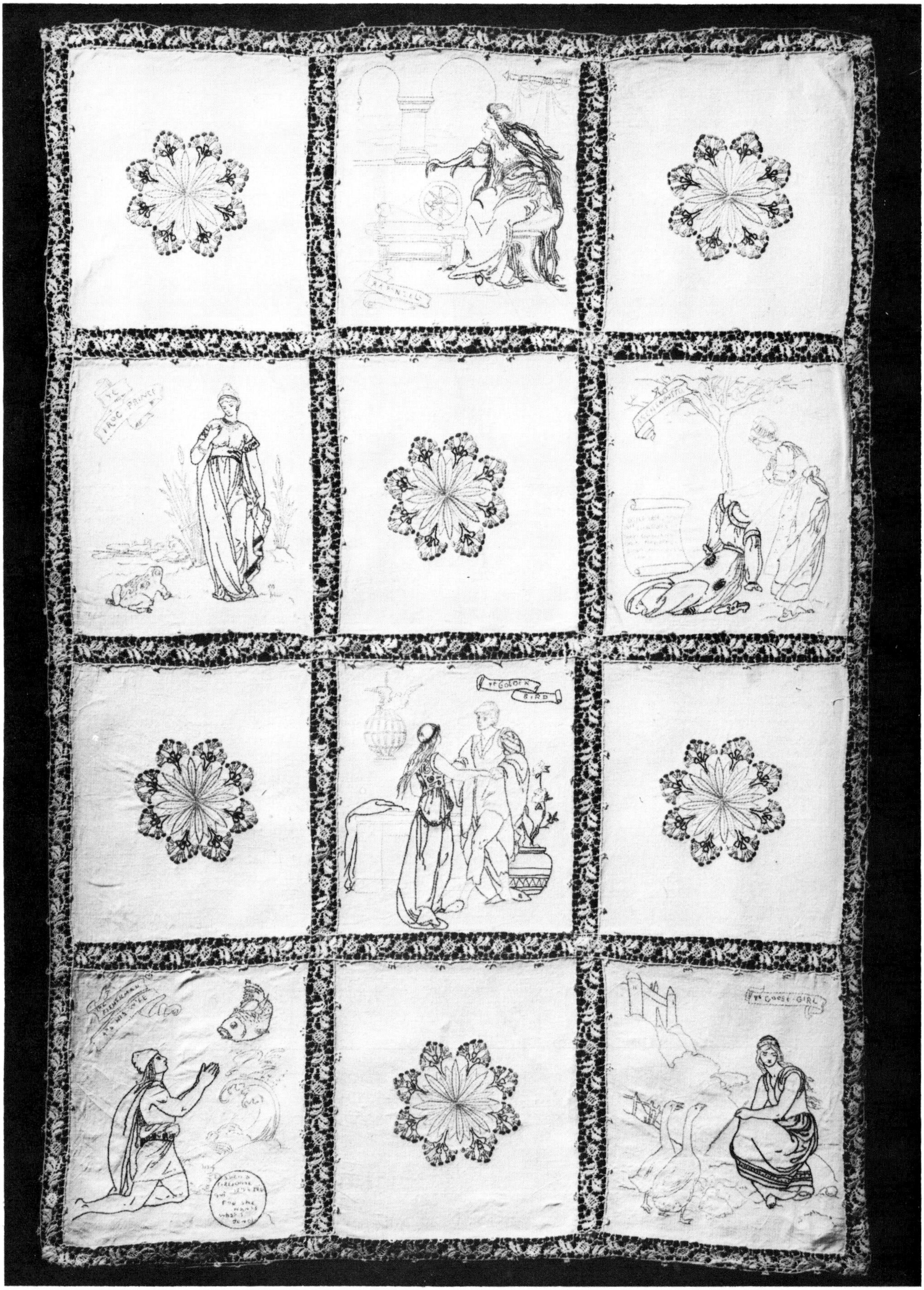
RAPUNZEL
YE FROG PRINCE
Ye GOLDEN BIRD
Ye GOOSE-GIRL

set to music (71). Widely admired, these illustrations for the nursery became the basis of his wallpaper designs, and were adapted for use as ceramic tiles as well as such items of handiwork as a beautifully embroidered cot cover and a set of doilies (117), (118).

The actual Toy book series was continued for Routledge by Randolph Caldecott who, like Crane, contributed two titles each Christmas. Caldecott was basically a caricaturist, but he was able to adapt his style to the nursery books without losing his sense of fun. His figures were less static than Crane's, for he was an artist used to depicting the flow and movement of the hunting field. Starting with *The House that Jack Built* and *John Gilpin*, he maintained the now established pattern of producing each year one book of nursery rhymes and one, a little more sophisticated, for older children. Caldecott's books sold in even greater numbers than Crane's, and new ones appeared each year until 1885 when the final pair: *Mrs Mary Blaize* and *The Great Panjandrum Himself*, the nonsense creature who was the potentate of all potentates, was published just a few months before Caldecott's death in Florida at the age of forty.

Kate Greenaway, the third of Evans's great illustrators, represented a further stage in the evolution of an aesthetic that began with William Morris and the Pre-Raphaelites. In her work, the sentiments of the courts of chivalry were re-enacted on the village green. Hers was a world of idealized children, obedient, immaculate and beautiful. Greenaway characters were visions of the Victorian ideal. They were tantalizing images that gave mothers wishful dreams of their own children that could never be realized, and gave the children themselves a responsibility, impossible to fulfil, of substantiating those dreams (86). The very unworldliness of her delphic trains of dancing children, hypnotized as if they were participants in some esoteric rite, gave them a timeless quality, and expressed a spirit of eternal childhood that was totally oblivious of the reality outside. In none of her illustrations do any of the children show the slightest smudge of dirt. There is no aggression, bumptiousness or loudness in her work for, like Edmund Evans, she abhorred the depiction of violence.

The Arcadian air that Kate Greenaway's children seemed to have was enhanced by the way she clothed them in the fashions that the French Revolution had introduced to Paris almost a century earlier, and which had spread throughout most of Europe. The miniature versions of adult clothing that had been the standard dress of children up to the time of the Revolution, were replaced by fashions more appropriate to their age. Embroidered silks were replaced by cottons with printed designs of minute flower heads tightly scattered over the whole fabric. Broad sashes, mob caps and slippers were worn, and it was these costumes, sensitively interpreted, that clothed Kate Greenaway's characters (67), (72).

Evans had always regarded himself as the owner of a colour-printing

117 (opposite) Walter Crane (after): cot cover, lace, *c.* 1895, Nottingham Museum of Costume & Textiles.

118 Walter Crane (after): doily, 'Bluebell' from 'Flora's Retinue', silk damask, manufactured by John Wilson & Sons, 1893. William Morris Gallery, London.

119 L. Leslie Brooke: 'The Yonghy Bonghy Bo', from *Nonsense Songs* by Edward Lear, Warne, 1900.

business in which wood engraving formed only a part. He had never considered founding a school of illustrators, but the engaging of talents sympathetic towards the principles he considered fit and suitable for children's books led to the development of a 'house style'. Its distinctiveness lay in the fact that all the printing was by wood engraving, which was essentially a linear rather than a tonal process. Craftsmen carved lines into blocks of wood in imitation of certain drawn lines, and the picture was built up of a play of these lines rather than as a harmonic gradation of tones. Linear perspective was simple to achieve, but tonal perspective was difficult, if not impossible. Furthermore, Evans limited the number of inks used at any stage, in order to preserve the freshness of the original illustration. Consequently, there was a similarity in the colouring of the work of his illustrators, even though, with experience, Evans was able to print the later books illustrated by Kate Greenaway in more subtle colours than the earlier ones by Walter Crane. In the case of all three of Evans's great artists an illustration was found to be more effective if it was divided into a foreground for the primary figures and a background for the secondary ones. Consequently, the 'encounter' situation – 'boy meets girl' or 'gentleman meets milkmaid', with the principal figures large and in the foreground, was a recognizable characteristic of the 'school', and was found even in the work of Leslie Brooke, one of the last of Evans's illustrators, who continued to draw in the same style until well into the 1930s (119).

Evans's nursery books were imported into the United States and were admired by local artists. The illustrations by Crane and Caldecott found a particular response in Howard Pyle, who was then at the beginning of his career. Pyle, later to become America's greatest illustrator, was in New York at the time, illustrating both fairy tales and stories of his own for the new children's magazines *Saint Nicholas*, *Harper's Weekly*, *Harper's Monthly* and *Scribner's Monthly*.

In 1881 Pyle was commissioned by the publishers Dodd Mead to illustrate an American equivalent of Evans's books. His magazine work had already shown the facility with which he could give character to faces and movement to figures and, as far as the artwork was concerned, the two books for Dodd Meade, *Yankee Doodle* and *The Lady of Shallott*, compared well with the British Toy books. *The Lady of Shallott* was drawn very much in the style of Crane's work, but it was *Yankee Doodle*, which owed more to Randolph Caldecott's work, that was better suited to Pyle's gifts. Here, the lively drawings stressed the bucolic nature of the characters, but the colours as printed were brash and strident, with vivid reds that gave noses and cheeks, especially those of General George Washington, an inebriated appearance (120). Pyle was so dissatisfied with the quality of the reproduction of his drawings that he abandoned the series and, unfortunately, never returned to this type of nursery book.

Of all Evans's illustrators, though, it was Kate Greenaway whose influence was the most far-reaching in both Britain and the United States. From her first book for Evans, *Under the Window* of 1878, to her last, *The April Baby's Book of Tunes* of 1900, a cult following developed that has lasted to the present day. Letter racks with Kate Greenaway motifs, china, cutlery with her characters moulded on the handles, and even buttons with figures from her actual or supposed illustrations, were manufactured. Wallpaper, bookplates, bookmarks and menus using Greenaway children as decorations were printed. Her greetings cards were on sale everywhere, and tiles after her designs were let into hearths and cabinets, or mounted in panels on the walls of innumerable nurseries. And all this, it must be remembered, without there being a single named Kate Greenaway character. She had invented a type and a style, but never a single personality. There was no 'Alice' and no 'Tom', just a fantasy land that all children could enter without any great financial outlay on the part of their parents.

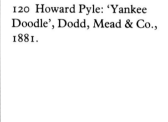

120 Howard Pyle: 'Yankee Doodle', Dodd, Mead & Co., 1881.

121 Mary Seddon Tyre: 'Oranges and Lemons', from *Children's Singing Games* by Alice B. Gomme, Nutt, 1894.

The Kate Greenaway dress had a long, if fitful influence on illustrators. Winifred Green and Mary Seddon Tyre (121), working in the 1890s, copied the style directly. Bertha Corbett's 'Sunbonnet Babies' (161) in the States at the turn of the century were contemporary reinterpretations, while Holly Hobbie and Tasha Tudor children (122) are modern recreations of the style. Greenaway fabrics are being worn again by children, and even *The Months* has reappeared, not this time on nursery walls but as wrapping paper.

In designing nursery tiles Kate Greenaway was working in a branch of decorative art that only became fashionable in the late Victorian age. Minton's, Doulton's, Maw's and Pilkington's all manufactured decorative tiles that could be inlaid into furniture or hung in panels on walls. Tiles were washable, permanent and attractive, and so were especially valuable in the nursery. Many beautiful transfer designs were created for these nursery tiles by staff designers of the companies themselves, as well as by independent professional illustrators. Scenes and characters from literature, fairy tales and nursery rhymes, as well as individual whimsical fancies, were produced in great quantities.

By the 1870s Walter Crane was designing tiles, for Maw's to have hand painted, using illustrations from his nursery books *The Baby's Opera* and *The Baby's Bouquet* as a basis (123). For some of the tiles he copied the illustrations directly, for others he showed the same scene as in the book, viewed from a different angle and, for yet others, he completely redrew his illustrations. It was a measure of the esteem in which Crane's work was held that the rival firm of Minton's was, at the same time, manufacturing tiles using equivalent designs copied directly from Crane's books by their own staff designers.

Kate Greenaway's tiles were designed by her for the firm of T. B. Boote. In a set of four, 'The Seasons', each tile, in delicate pinks and greys, showed one of her young ladies in the appropriate dress for that particular time of year. An unusual set, using illustrations taken from her *Birthday Book* of 1880, had tiles quartered and divided by overlapping bands of decoration, very much like Japanese Imari ware, which gave them an Art Deco appearance long before that movement began (124).

A number of tiles existed 'after' Kate Greenaway in which, like Walter Crane's and as had happened with the wallpapers, scenes were made up of a number of characters taken from different illustrations. Another group of tiles illustrating nursery rhymes and stories were manufactured in the 1880s by Minton's and, although not copied from Greenaway figures, show the influence of her work. Red Riding Hood was given the

122 (above) Tasha Tudor: 'Expectation', pen and ink, 1979. Private collection.

123 (left) Nursery tile: 'Little Boy Blue', designed by Walter Crane, Maw & Co., *c.* 1875; 6 in. square. Ironbridge Gorge Museum Trust.

124 Nursery tile, after Kate Greenaway, Minton Hollins & Co., *c.* 1885; 6 in. square. Collection of H. van Lemmen.

coquettishly sigmoid stance of a Greenaway sylph, while Miss Muffett, in a beautifully composed design, was shown overshadowed by an immense spider's web, as if in a science fiction version of the rhyme (C24), (125).

One of the finest designers of tiles of the period was J. Moyr Smith, whose work was reminiscent of Crane's. He produced a beautiful series of fairy tale tiles for Minton's, each with the illustration set imaginatively in a circular framework within the square tile. These, together with the intricate Walter Scott tiles that were used in the nursery of the Mill Owner's House at Bradford, show a feeling for the subject and a mastery of form that were completely in keeping with the Arts and Crafts principles he subscribed to (24).

The greatest ceramicist of the age, though, and a fine exponent of the art of the tile was William De Morgan. In the 1890s he designed for the nursery a number of delightful tiles using his own transfers and stencils of animals both extant and extinct. His dodo and his Bambi-like gazelle (126) were based on forms in Persian art, but they had a whimsicality that was entirely original, and showed the changes in technique and taste that had taken place since the 1870s when, for example, at the beginning of the

125 (above) Nursery tiles: J. Moyr Smith for Minton, transfer printed and hand painted, date unknown; 6 in. square. Gladstone Pottery Museum.

126 (right) Nursery tile: 'Gazelle' by William De Morgan, *c.* 1880; 6 in. square. William Morris Gallery.

fashion, Thomas Allen had designed a set of Aesop Fable tiles for Minton's (127).

The vogue for nursery tiles lasted barely twenty-five years and ended with remarkable suddenness at the turn of the century. In more modern times artists have occasionally used plain tiles on which to paint their own designs. Jessie M. King, in 1906, decorated a panel of tiles with illustrations in lilac of 'Ride a-Cock Horse', and Charles Voysey in the 'thirties used some of his 'Alice' designs for nursery tiles, but the decorative tile had fallen out of favour and, with the notable exception of the Dunsmore tiles of Beatrix Potter characters, few were produced commercially. Not until the 1950s and the time of the Festival of Britain did they reappear, no longer for inlays in furniture, but as an example of the revived spirit of British craftsmanship, to be admired and displayed in the nursery as artistic objects in their own right.

127 Nursery tile: 'The Hare and the Tortoise' by Thomas Allen, from *Aesop's Fables*, for Minton, *c.* 1885; 6 in. square. Gladstone Pottery Museum.

CHAPTER 8

Anthropomorphism

Although Crane, Caldecott and Greenaway wrote and illustrated many beautiful books for children, nowhere did they manage to create a single character, as the Uptons did with Golliwogg, that was able to capture the hearts of all children. Achievement such as this happens rarely. It seems to take place fortuitously, and appears to be independent of the quality of the work. Florence Upton was only a minor illustrator, and Bertha Upton hardly a significant writer of verse, yet Golliwogg was a complete success.

The basic requirement is that such a character should have the potential to become a projection of the child or of somebody close to him. It should relate to the child's environment or his pattern of behaviour, and should exaggerate some aspects of these. Ideally it should be a possible playmate for the child: one that is approximately his own age and size. Its adventures, like Golly's or Pinocchio's should be within the compass of the child's imagination, so that the child could live those adventures vicariously. Above all, the technique and inventiveness of the artist should provide a pictorial image with sufficient impact to stimulate the child's imagination.

The best of these characters have been animals, especially those which could be made to walk on their hind legs and be given facial expressions to match human ones. There should be some realistic element to allow the child to make initial contact, but not so great a realism as to lessen the originality of the new image. This is the weakness of Louis Wain's somewhat overrated cats (128), or even the illustrations of the anthropomorphic railway engines in the Reverend Awdry's admirable books. In *Peter Pan*, that casebook for psychology enthusiasts, neither Mabel

Lucie Attwell, F.D. Bedford nor Flora White were able to portray Nana, the dog, convincingly in their illustrations for the scenes with the Darling children (87). Only Walt Disney's conception of the relationship between dog and humans has been a feasible one, and here only because the nature of the medium he used converted all the characters into cartoon figures. For the same reason there is no definitive 'Black Beauty' because Black Beauty is always portrayed naturalistically. In America, the very realistic 'Billy Whiskers', the goat that Arthur DeBebian illustrated for Frances Montgomery's stories, would be unrecognizable out of context. On the other hand, Mickey Mouse who is no mouse really but a unique product of creation, can become a projection of the child. He is, in effect, a small boy with a licence to do things and, moreover, possessing the wherewithal to succeed, that a child in the nursery would envy.

For anthropomorphism to be effective, especially in exciting or humorous situations, caricature is essential. And there must be a name, no matter how simple. 'Mole' or 'Peter Rabbit' are not the most original or memorable names, but the characters, by being named, have been given individual personalities, and the child is then able to establish a rapport with them.

Beatrix Potter was one of the first to give this identity to many of the hitherto anonymous animals that had always been nursery favourites. The very names she gave them, together with a few well-chosen characteristics and a minimum of props, turned Squirrel Nutkin, Jemima Puddle-duck, Mrs Tiggy-winkle and so many others, into individuals whom children over the years have recognized as friends. The genius of her story-telling ensured that the whole of her art, despite certain incongruities, was accepted unreservedly. Baby rabbits, for example, were allowed to be unclothed but male rabbits, although trouserless, had to wear jackets, and lady rabbits were never seen without being correctly dressed in ankle-length skirts. Nevertheless, Peter Rabbit and his friends have appeared in more editions and have taken form in the nursery in more ways than any other children's characters. Every gift shop in Britain has a selection of Beatrix Potter animals decorating tableware, birthday books and diaries, as well as wall pictures, friezes and pottery models (129), (130).

The watercolours in the Peter Rabbit books recreated the freshness of spring or the heat of a summer's day with a shimmer that was often reminiscent of an Impressionist painting. When visitors to Hill Top Farm, Beatrix Potter's home in the Lake District, see the reality, it is as if a telescope has been turned round. Everything is small and finite. The world of the Flopsy Bunnies is encompassable in a very few strides, while inside the house are laid out, row upon row, those beautiful watercolours that are testimony to the genius of the artist and her ability to see eternity in a square yard of garden. It is not surprising how few imitators Beatrix Potter had. In terms of artwork, only Margaret Tempest's illustrations

128 Louis Wain: 'The Pussy-cats' Barber' from *The Infant's Magazine*, Partridge & Co., 1896.

c24 (opposite above left) Nursery tile, 'Miss Muffet', Minton, *c.* 1880. Collection of Gladstone Pottery Museum, Stoke-on-Trent.

c25 (opposite above right) L.D. Bradley: *Our Indians*, Dutton, New York, 1899.

c26 (opposite below) Pop-up book. *The Daily Express Children's Annual* no. 5, Lane Publications, London, 1935.

for Alison Uttley's *Little Grey Rabbit* books and Barbara Vernon's lively 'Bunnykins' designs for Doulton's nursery china, could be considered worthy successors to Beatrix Potter's distinctive style (131), (132).

129 Nursery wallpaper after Beatrix Potter, manufactured by Shand Kydd, 1977. © Frederick Warne PLC.

130 Nursery tea set after Beatrix Potter, Wedgwood & Co. © Frederick Warne PLC.

Beatrix Potter's interpretation of both her stories and her illustrations was relatively realistic. In general, though, animal adventures in nursery art have been depicted by caricature. Distortion and exaggeration help to widen the scope of drawing facial expressions and movement, but caricature is a method that has to be used with caution when drawing for children because the boundaries of plausibility are soon crossed. The Australian illustrator Dorothy Wall was particularly successful in balancing realism with caricature in her drawings of 'Blinky Bill' (133), the koala

C27 William Denslow: 'Rock-a-bye-baby' from *Mother Goose*, McLuire, Philadelphia, 1901.

131 (above and left) Barbara Vernon: designs for 'Bunnykins' ware, Doulton, 1936.

132 (centre left) Barbara Vernon: 'Bunnykins' ware, Doulton.

bear. She was helped by the fact that a koala bear is already a caricature of a baby, being small and cuddly, with a round face to which an artist can add expression without undue distortion. Like most successful illustrators of animal stories she was able to blend the natural attributes of her animals with more flexible human ones.

Harry Rountree, a prolific illustrator who specialized in squat, rather chunky birds and animals – it was he who drew the sensitive doormouse advertisements for Mansion polish and Cherry Blossom boot polish – was a perfect exponent of this. His characterization was exemplary. He left his animals in their natural surroundings but gave them a range of expression sufficient to let them reveal the shyness, cheekiness or disconcertment that made them so endearing. His success lay in the fact that their adventures,

"Little bear," he cried softly, "it is too light for me to see farther."

133 (above) Dorothy Wall: '"Little bear," he cried softly', from *Blinky Bill Grows Up*, © Angus & Robertson Publishers, Sydney, 1934.

134 (right) Ernest Aris: 'Little Mousie Crusoe' from the book by May Byron, Cassell & Co., 1923.

and their responses to the situations, were inflated pictures of what might really happen when, for example, a bough broke or a little mouse was left marooned on an island. He never attempted a gross distortion of nature by dressing up his animals in golfing outfits or putting them in motor cars, as Ernest Aris, another popular nursery illustrator of the 'twenties, did in the mouse stories he wrote. Aris brought his characters into the world of humans. He had them attend school, go shopping, and even undergo the mouse equivalent of the adventures of Robinson Crusoe (134). That said, he was honest within his terms of reference. He blended caricature and realism in such a way as to preserve many of the animal characteristics and, although he lacked the purity of Rountree's approach, he kept the behaviour of his characters within the framework of human experience.

135 Lancing Campbell: 'He had an umbrella', from *Uncle Wiggily's Story Book* by Howard R. Garis, A.L. Burt Co., New York, 1921.

Still further removed from the animal environment was Howard Garis's eccentric American rabbit 'Uncle Wiggily' who, in Lancing Campbell's illustrations, was given a top hat and a frock coat. Like the majority of animals in children's books and comics, he was really a human in disguise and underwent adventures of a purely human kind. He lived in a cottage, drove a motor car, and was really a caricature of everybody's 'crazy old gentleman down the road' (135).

All anthropomorphic animals were, of course, humans in fancy dress. The great characters of children's comics, Teddy Tail, Tiger Tim or

136 (opposite) Arthur Rackham: 'It was a golden afternoon', from *The Wind in the Willows* by Kenneth Grahame, pen, ink and watercolour, The Limited Editions Club, New York, 1939.

Bobby Bruin, were all transference forms of their little readers who, through them, could act out the life of their dreams undetected in their animal disguise. They could be made to endure hardships that no child could cope with. They could be made to take part in escapades for which small children knew they could expect punishment if they were caught. Through them the child could experience the supreme joy of outwitting grown-ups. Anthropomorphism offered a world of everlasting play and mischief untroubled by nannies or parents. Molly Brett, who had been one of the artists of the 'Fairy School' in the 1920s, later foresook her little pixies for scenes of teddy bears and animals at play. She invented a never-never land of disguised children in blissful abandon, happy and safe (84). Her art never seemed fully stretched by the demands made on it, but it always had an immediate appeal for children, and no nursery school today would be complete without its reproduction of a Molly Brett picture on the wall.

The most beautiful expression of anthropomorphism in all literature has been Kenneth Grahame's *The Wind in the Willows*. When the book first appeared in 1908 its only illustration was a small vaguely atmospheric frontispiece by W. Graham Robertson. The famous drawings by Ernest Shepard were not, in fact, done until almost a quarter of a century later. Originally Arthur Rackham had been invited by the author to provide illustrations for the first edition but, owing to pressure of work, he had declined the offer. It was a decision he regretted for many years until, in 1939, for what was to be his last work, he illustrated the book for George Macey's Limited Editions Club of New York.

Ernest Shepard's black and white illustrations of 1931 conveyed the feel of the story so successfully that it was difficult to conceive of any other way of illustrating the book. Shepard understood perfectly Mole's sheer joy at being alive at the coming of spring. Drawing after drawing showed his complete sympathy with Grahame's story, and they were not to be equalled until Rackham, as he had done thirty years earlier for *Alice in Wonderland*, was able to give the work a new and equally valid set of images.

Rackham's sensitive treatment of 'It was a golden afternoon' demonstrated his solution to one of the problems of anthropomorphism: that of how to balance animals of different sizes against a man-made apparatus that relates to an altogether different scale of measurements. Rackham reduced the size of the caravan, slightly enlarged the figures of Toad and Rat behind it, and controlled the proportions by having the horse bend down towards Mole and so reduce the disparity between their sizes (136). Shepard, on the other hand, tried to remain true to the natural size of the little animals, and left the reader posing the question of how such tiny creatures could manipulate such a large vehicle (137). No illustrator of *The Wind in the Willows* seems to have offered the simplest solution of all.

137 Ernest Shepard: 'Toad sat straight down . . .', from *The Wind in the Willows* by Kenneth Grahame, Methuen & Co., 1931. © 1933 Charles Scribner's Sons; © renewed 1961 Ernest H. Shepard. Reprinted with the permission of Methuen & Co. Ltd. and Charles Scribner's Sons.

Using the basic fact of perspective that nearer objects look larger, it should be possible to draw the friends from a low viewpoint in the foreground, and so make them in proportion to the caravan in the background.

The one Australian book with an original character of equivalent impact did not appear until 1918 when Norman Lindsay's *The Magic Pudding* was published. Lindsay, a sort of antipodean Hemingway, was an illustrator by profession before he became a writer. *The Magic Pudding* was a noisy outdoor tale told in a breezy manner with frequent interludes for the characters to burst out into catchy rum-ti-tum songs. The humorous illustrations, drawn in *conte*, matched the pace and liveliness of the story in which the hero was not so much the Magic Pudding himself as his friend Mr Bunyip Bluegum, a Koala Bear of Leisure (138). Lindsay was surprised and disappointed to find that the work for which he had become famous was this one book he had written for children, but *The Magic Pudding* is unlike any other children's book ever written and is the first to come to mind when Australian nursery stories are mentioned. It bears claim to be considered one of the great classics of children's literature.

Anthropomorphism, whether of Bunyip Bluegum or the caterpillar in

Alice has the advantage to the illustrator of allowing him to depict fantasy. It is much more difficult to be original when drawing animals in a naturalistic manner. Animal pictures have been part of an infant's education ever since the very first of John Newbery's children's books was published in the middle of the eighteenth century. Every nursery child has at least one picture of a cow, a lamb or a farmyard rooster. The term 'our four-footed friends' is more than a poetic metaphor; it is the expression of one of the levels of the nursery hierarchy. Pets are members of the family, a little lower in pecking order than the child, but on hand to be offered affection when the mood requires, or abuse when the going gets rough.

There is a sameness about 'farmyard art' that comes from the inhibiting strictures of naturalistic interpretation. The illustrations are usually portraits of the animals, with captions and minimal text, designed to teach the very youngest children animal recognition. The pictures are occasionally livened up by having group scenes with different types of animals browsing together in harmony. As artists through the ages have found, it is very difficult to achieve originality without distortion. Perhaps only the Detmold brothers found a truly satisfactory solution by setting the accurately representational creatures they drew in lyrical dream-like landscapes (139).

Farmyard pictures are one of the few aspects of nursery art where the old fashioned principles of didacticism in the nursery have persisted. Despite the revolutionary changes that the animated cartoon has made in the nursery iconography, the realistic approach towards teaching children their animals has never been superseded. It is often dull art, but nothing more convincing has yet been found. Didacticism and factual reality are often unfortunate and necessary participants in the process of leading the child out of the shelter of the nursery and into the world outside.

138 Norman Lindsay: '"You're a bun-headed old optimist," said the Pudding', from *The Magic Pudding*, Angus & Robertson Ltd., Sydney, 1918; © Janet Glad, 1916.

139 Edward Julius Detmold: 'The Fawn', from *The Book of Baby Beasts* by Florence E. Dugdale, Hodder & Stoughton, 1911.

CHAPTER 9

Humour in Art for the Nursery

The division of animal illustrations into the naturalistic and the caricatured merely acknowledged the fact that nursery art in the nineteenth century had taken two main paths. In one, illustrators adapted contemporary trends in fine art to the decoration of books. In the other, the line was swift and the images simplified, with drawings that had the vitality and spontaneity of the more ephemeral world of the cartoonist. By the latter part of the century children's comic papers had begun to appear, and it was in these publications that caricature and the zestful energy of this more spontaneous art came into its own.

From the outset, comics in the United States differed from those in Great Britain. In the United States they were issued as coloured supplements in newspapers and, automatically, commanded a vast readership. In Britain they were independent weekly publications. The British comics had originally been intended solely for adults, and the view that their contents were vulgar and corruptive persisted long after their total metamorphosis into children's comics. The first children's paper to have comic strips, *The Rainbow*, did not begin publication until as late as 1914, and not until 1920, with *Chic's Own*, did there appear a comic paper for the very young in which every syllable was hyphenated to help those who were just beginning to read.

In British newspapers the comic was confined to a single black and white strip in each daily issue. The first of these was Charles Folkard's 'Teddy Tail', which started in the *Daily Mail* in 1914, and was soon followed by J.F. Horrabin's 'The Noah Family' in the *Daily News* (140). Austin Payne's 'Pip, Squeak and Wilfred' began in the *Daily Mirror* in

1921 and, shortly afterwards, the one comic strip that has remained virtually unchanged to this day appeared in the *Daily Express*: 'Rupert and his Friends', drawn initially by Mary Tourtel.

In scope, presentation and sophistication the comic strips in the British newspapers could not compare with their American counterparts. Their strength lay in their charm and lack of aggressiveness. The British characters tended to relate to a child-orientated world, whereas American comics portrayed the child in relation to the adult world. British comics had more animals: i.e. children in animal dress; American comics had more off-beat kids such as R.F. Outcault's 'The Yellow Kid' or his notorious 'Buster Brown' (141).

The adventures of Buster Brown and his faithful dog Tige, which first appeared in 1902 as a colour supplement in the *New York Herald*, had an enormous following of wishfully inclined children. Churchmen, who considered the strip a banner from Hell, frowned, but parents, by and large, came to accept Buster's irresistible appeal. He was ten years old, came from a wealthy family and therefore, although a rebel in his social class, was not beyond hope.

Here we see Mr. Cheery paying a call on the Noahs. He's telling them a most interesting piece of news—MOST interesting! He's got tired, he says, of being a lonely old bachelor, so he's decided to adopt a little boy to live with him; and the little boy is due to arrive immediately. The Noahs were tremendously excited.

1

140 J.F. Horrabin: 'Joy at the Ark', from *The Noah Family*, Cassell & Co. Ltd., 1922.

141 R.F. Outcault: 'Buster Brown tries raising chickens', from *The New York Herald*, 1903.

Books of Buster Brown's escapades appeared, and both he and Tige became famous throughout the United States. The success of the characters supported a whole industry of goods, ranging from picture postcards to Buster Brown Alphabet Plates and money boxes, all produced under licence from the Outcault Advertising Company of Chicago that was directed, with astute farsightedness, by the illustrator himself. The very clothes that Buster Brown wore, the dancing class shoes and the 'Buster Suit' with its belted smock, bow tie and bloomers (itself adapted from the 'Little Lord Fauntleroy' suit) was adopted by parents and hated by little boys on both sides of the Atlantic. In the windows of certain shoe shops stood a large cut-out figure of Tige signifying that Buster Brown shoes could be bought there.

In the United States there was less distinction between illustrators for comics and those for nursery books and, around the turn of the century, examples of both styles could be found in both types of publication. L.D. Bradley, a cartoonist on the *Chicago Daily News*, whose brilliant work for the nursery is now sadly overlooked, illustrated two books in cartoon style that Dutton published in 1899. In both *Wonderful Willie*, which dealt with the adventures of a little boy at the time of the Spanish American war, and *Our Indians*, the art work was comic art: simple, bold and funny (C25). Both books show Bradley to have been quite undeserving of this neglect, and to have been far more talented than the more celebrated Outcault, much of whose work was crudely drawn.

One of the earliest books to combine both types of illustration was *Yankee Mother Goose*, illustrated in 1902 by Ella S. Brison. At each corner of the title page was a realistic goose pecking at Art Nouveau loops of thread which formed a loosely woven border to the drawing. In the centre was a large cartoon of a goose dressed in a strange mixture of Tam-o'-Shanter and poncho, roller-skating across the page (142). The contrast between the brash central image and the wit and elegance of the border was original and effective, and by no means as incongruous as might have been expected.

The distortions of reality that were the ingredients of the humorous books extended to the actual shape and manner in which some of the books were constructed. Novelty books for children had been common since the middle of the eighteenth century, and movable books with rotating discs for carrying out astrological predictions had, in fact, been known since Renaissance times. Rebus books, with their symbolic representation of syllables – an 'eye' for an 'I' – had long been in use in nurseries

142 Ella S. Brison: title page for *Yankee Mother Goose* by Benjamin F. Cobb, Jamieson-Higgins Co., 1902.

to stimulate interest in religious teaching. The true 'trick' books appeared in the nursery for the first time in the 1850s. They incorporated many ingenious devices: sliding panels which, when moved, revealed new illustrations; pages cut into horizontal strips so that fabulous beasts could be made up of sections of different animals; and pictures with tabs or levers which, when pulled, allowed a portion of the illustration to move, so that Moses, for instance, could be made to float out of the bullrushes in a tiny basket. Shaped books were made in the form of dolls, animals, soldiers and sailors. A series of 'Furry' books featured animals with coats made of real hair or wool flock. There were books which unfolded to make a complete panorama of a procession or scenic view. Books existed which, by flipping the finger up or down the edge of the pages, would make moving pictures in which Humpty Dumpty could be made either to fall off his wall, or defy all the stories and be put together again. Pop-up books were made in many imaginative and complex forms, from a single figure that stood up as the book was opened, to intricate theatrical assemblages of cottages, trees and flowers and numerous characters, all set out in tiers (C26). Advent calendars, with window-flaps that were to be lifted one a day before Christmas, offered opportunities to an inventive artist to create wonders for the nursery. Drawing books were printed with apparently blank pages over which a child could scribble in pencil to reveal a hidden picture or, more impressively, turn a sponge into a magic wand which, when swept over the page, could produce beautiful coloured pictures. Even more sophisticated was the 'Snow White Magic Mirror Book' in which blurred pictures of the Seven Dwarfs took on a striking three-dimensional appearance when looked at through the cardboard spectacles which accompanied the book.

The search for novelty in nursery books took many forms, not least in the work of the American, Peter Newell, whose genius as an inventor of clever and amusing books was exceptional. Newell manipulated the very physical nature of the nursery book. He played with the rectangularity, the thickness and the conventions of the right and wrong way up, with the freedom of a sculptor, the magic of a conjuror and the humour of a music hall entertainer. In the early years of the century he established himself as the supreme exponent of the 'Trick' book.

Newell was a book illustrator with a sense of fun, rather than a cartoonist with a desire to escape from the world of the comic newspapers. In both his *Alice in Wonderland* of 1901 and *Alice Through the Looking Glass* of 1902 he showed an ability to rethink the illustrations without reference to his predecessors, making, for example, the Red Queen a carved wooden chess piece with clothes on. His earliest trick book, *Topsys and Turveys* of 1894, employed a familiar device of comic illustration with pictures that could be changed by turning the page upside down. *A Shadow Show*, published in New York in 1896, had pages which revealed funny faces when held up against the light. In 1910 Newell designed his rhombus-shaped *The Slant Book* which used the distorted angulation of the book to provide ready-made hills down which the objects in the illustrations were supposed to roll out of control with disastrous results.

143 Peter Newell: *The Hole Book*, Harper Bros., New York, 1908.

Newell's most famous book, *The Hole Book*, published in 1908, described on the first page how a gun, which little Tom Pot was playing with, accidentally went off. Each page had an actual hole in it to show where the bullet had passed, with the characters in each episode looking with astonishment at the damage, none of it serious, it had just caused. On its travels, the bullet pierced Dick Bumble's bag of grain, to the joy of the hens who gobbled it up; it shattered Granny Fink's goldfish bowl and perforated the big drum of the town band to the consternation of the bandsmen (143). With this book, and its companion *The Rocket Book*, which dealt in a similar manner with the adventures of a firework, Peter Newell brought the art of the trick book to a level that has never been surpassed.

By the end of the nineteenth century, the pattern of social life in Britain had begun to change. Tastes had begun to diffuse in both directions across

144 John Hassall: 'Three Men in a Tub', from *Popular Nursery Rhymes*, Blackie & Sons, 1921.

hitherto impenetrable class barriers, and the stifling religiosity of the earlier Victorian days began to show signs of weakening its hold on the family. Acknowledgment of the very existence of the profane was felt to be less of a sign of being possessed by Satan. Phil May's 'Guttersnipes' came to be looked upon as an amusing feature of the social scene rather than as apprentice criminals, and a more colloquial and earthy humour became more generally acceptable. This new tendency towards egalitarianism encouraged the development of a new style of humorous art that soon reached the nursery, both in the comic papers and in the work of those gentlemen who gathered each week at the London Sketch Club.

Many important children's illustrators – René Bull, Frank Reynolds, Heath Robinson and Edmund Dulac among them – were members of the London Sketch Club: a society that had been formed to allow graphic artists to mix with their fellows, exchange ideas and, above all, practise their art in convivial surroundings. Mainly through the work of John Hassall and Cecil Aldin the art of the 'Smoking Concert' became the art of the nursery. Hassall illustrated over one hundred children's books and, in addition, many single pictures for magazine illustration or for wall decoration, all in an unmistakable style that was both original and humorous (144). He introduced both the sugarloaf hat that was later worn by some of Mabel Lucie Attwell's characters, and the little mongrel dog that was adopted as a feature by his friend Cecil Aldin who was to become as much the artist of 'the dog' as Louis Wain was the artist of 'the cat'.

Humorous art, like Hassall's or Heath Robinson's, is much more direct than the somewhat self-conscious art of Florence Harrison or Jessie M. King. The more serious the art the more durable it is expected to be. Fine art is looked upon as being necessarily remote. It is something precious and to be kept. Humorous art, because it is less esoteric, its presentation less ornate and its joys more ephemeral, is usually considered to be a lesser art. However, the greatest illustrators for the nursery were able to adapt their style to the nature of the text. Mabel Lucie Attwell stood as a gigantic talent of great versatility who could illustrate *The Water Babies* (94), *Peter Pan* and *Alice in Wonderland*, as well as the adventures of the 'Boo-Boos' (C10). Heath Robinson illustrated *Tales from Hans Christian Andersen* as well as his own *Uncle Lubin* which, beneath its cartoon-like appearance, was a masterpiece of form, drawn with the utmost simplicity (145). His superb technique was combined with fantastic flights of imagination, and his genius for introducing little incidentals to the main theme has been matched only by Edmund Dulac's. In Uncle Lubin's ascent in the balloon, the frayed string with its knot, the indentation made by the hat, and the idea of having a Gladstone bag for the sandwiches, were all marvels of invention. Every large drawing on the right hand page was echoed by one or more secondary drawings on the left, each one telling a little more about the story. Above all, Heath Robinson's drawings were funny. They showed, in their ability to delight and cajole children, his true understanding of the art of the nursery book.

William Denslow, in the United States, shared Heath Robinson's understanding of how to illustrate effectively for the nursery. Denslow was an artist on a Chicago newspaper, and his line, like Heath Robinson's, was solid and sought clarity rather than subtlety, although he was well able to soften any harshness that might have intruded into a drawing by introducing wispy arabesques of Art Nouveau. His style was light-hearted and mischievous as in the *Mother Goose* he illustrated in 1901 with its happy American Indian 'Rock-a-bye-Baby' (C27). It was Denslow who first gave form to Frank Baum's *The Wonderful Wizard of Oz*. His were the first incarnations of the Lion, the Tin Man, the Scarecrow and, above all, Dorothy who, for a long time, was small and chunky, until the Denslow image was replaced for evermore, thirty-nine years later, by the young Judy Garland (146).

Great illustration for the nursery does not depend on the voice the artist uses, whether serious or comic, but on how readily he can adapt to the nature of the text. More than pity and fellow feeling, the child responds to humour, because the mark of childhood is egocentricity, and humour is an emotion that is extended towards the child. Pity is what the child would have to give of himself, and that is very much more difficult. For

145 W. Heath Robinson: *Uncle Lubin*, Grant Richards, 1902; © 1932 Estate of Mrs J.C. Robinson. © Puffin Books.

ALL next day the sorrowful Lubin racked his brain to find a way of rescuing little Peter. At last he decided to build an Air-ship, and he set about the work at once.
In a few days the ship was finished, and Uncle Lubin was able to start on his voyage.
Towards midnight he got quite near the moon, and found the wicked Bag-bird perched upon it.
12

both these reasons Kay Nielsen, for example, or even Virginia Sterrett, although very great illustrators of children's Gift books, were not great illustrators for the nursery (C31). Their work was beautiful but remote. The nursery illustrator has to come to the child and not expect the child to learn to appreciate the artistic merit of his offerings. Nursery art has its own special problems. Its simplicity is deceptive. It is not naïve art, and illustrating for the nursery should never be looked upon as a refuge for the less able. Bad art, even naïve art, is the product of either the unsophisticated, the inept or the cunning. It takes genius to achieve the simplicity that is the prerequisite of great nursery art.

146 William Denslow: 'You ought to be ashamed of yourself', from *The Wonderful Wizard of Oz* by Frank L. Baum, George M. Hill, Chicago, 1900.

CHAPTER 10

Art Nouveau in the Nursery

The illustrated book provided one of the very few forms in which Art Nouveau was to be found in the nursery. As a decorative art movement its main expression was in objects that often sacrificed function for appearance, and hence were not always practical for nursery needs. Art Nouveau furniture, fabrics and utensils, with their hysteresis curves and inability to stay still, were designed for an adult world. In the nursery, other than as pictures on the walls or between the covers of books, Art Nouveau was largely limited to the occasional adventurously designed christening set or decorated tile. Nevertheless, when its principles were correctly assimilated, it became for the artist more a way of seeing than a means of embellishing an image. It gave the illustrator a greater flexibility of expression in both line and form. Its greatest exponents used it not only to create graceful shapes, but to serve a structural purpose by uniting disparate sections and compelling the viewer to follow a picture in the way the artist wanted. Charles Robinson and Mabel Lucie Attwell used it to decorate the book itself, taking it beyond the illustrations to the enhancement of the whole page. With Arthur Rackham, the whirlwinds of excited line became so natural that they ended up not an outcome of illustration but a tool of expression.

Charles Robinson's art linked that of William Morris and Walter Crane with Art Nouveau. Morris's preference of vine leaves and acanthus leaves as decoration was taken up by Arthur Gaskin and his fellow members of the Birmingham School of Design, as well as Arthur Rackham himself (147). The emergence of Art Nouveau gradually let light into this dense foliage whilst, at the same time, retaining the interesting waves of its form.

147 Georgie France: 'Little Jack Horner' from *A Book of Nursery Songs and Rhymes* by S. Baring Gould, Methuen, 1895.

Not every swirl makes an artist a practitioner of Art Nouveau, nor does every simplification of black and white into plain contrasting masses signify a disciple of Aubrey Beardsley but, through the work of Charles Robinson, the new ideas that were influencing the art of the book reached the nursery. By 1896, in *The Child World*, Robinson was already transforming heavy leaves into sinuous tendrils that curled round cartouches, and formed loops and whorls round the rectangular borders, so that the illustrations seemed to have been given the importance of pictures framed on a wall.

148 Charles Robinson: 'Siesta', pen and ink, *c.* 1927; 12 in. × 20½ in. Private collection.

In many ways the roly-poly babies that Charles Robinson drew were the ancestors of Mabel Lucie Attwell's and Ernest Shepard's, but he also recognized the cunning of children, and understood the ease with which they could manipulate the hearts of grown-ups. By the beginning of the century he had abandoned the darker side of his art and eliminated any disturbing undertones so that, until his death in 1936, the clean linear style of, for example, the beautiful nursery drawing 'Siesta', predominated and hardly altered in his work (148).

Charles Robinson's counterpart in the United States was Howard Pyle. Like Robinson's, his art straddled the period between the more formal Arts and Crafts type of decoration and the looser forms that came to overtake it. After his unhappy experience with the Toy books, Pyle's books for younger children were largely anthologies of tales he himself had written and illustrated, mainly for *Harper's Young People* (149). He and Robinson possessed the same gift for simplicity. His *Pepper and Salt* of 1886, with its sinewy heroes with elfin chins and pointed noses, showed how advanced he was in omitting borders from his illustrations in order to allow them to be better integrated with the text. Like Charles Robinson he possessed the remarkable ability to use large blank areas of his drawing to balance the decorated ones. He could also, like Robinson, alternate between a swift light line and a heavier, almost sculptural one that he employed for his stories for older children. Only in *The Wonder Clock* of 1888 did he use the heavier style in a nursery book and this, significantly, was the only book of his whose illustrations were known to have upset little children (37). Pyle was a superb draughtsman and, although most of his work as a book illustrator – and this includes the best 'Robin Hood' there has ever been – was for older children, he was one of the few artists who could draw equally well for both the nursery and the schoolroom.

The most important of the illustrators whose art covered the period that spanned the rise and fall of Art Nouveau was Arthur Rackham. Rackham, who could draw anything, produced matchless examples of wit and pathos, rumbustiousness and serenity, beauty and grotesqueness, all without apparent effort.

In the late 1890s Rackham abandoned the realistic type of illustration that he had been practising for the previous decade, in favour of the freer and more fantastic style that he had always preferred, and in which he illustrated the many children's books for which he became famous. Nowadays, his work is so familiar that one hardly pauses to consider it in the context of the art of its time. Rackham was a generous artist, and his books are studded with goblins, mermaids, elves and monsters. Many were drawn in the recognizable looped and curled forms of Art Nouveau. Others, with their heavy surrounds of foliage in dense black and white, show the earlier influence of William Morris. We recognize them as 'Rackhams' and overlook the fact that the style was an acquired one and that, for the most part, these fascinating drawings were his own interpretation of Art Nouveau.

In both silhouette and line Arthur Rackham made trees talk and fairies become our own personal familiars. He gave arthritic witches and edentulous old men an ennobling grace. No other illustrator has ever inspired a poem, as has Rackham from John Betjeman. No other book illustration has ever been the model for a piece of music, as has Rackham's 'Fairies are Exquisite Dancers' from *Peter Pan in Kensington Gardens* for one of Debussy's Preludes for piano. Rackham illustrated all the classic children's books: *Andersen*, *Grimm*, *Alice*, *The Wind in the Willows* (but, surprisingly, no *Water Babies*). Any slight changes of style that could be

149 Howard Pyle: 'Claus and the Master of Black Arts', from *Pepper and Salt*, Harper & Bros, New York, 1886.

detected over the years were developmental rather than exploratory; a little more black in the watercolours here, a greater calligraphic freedom there, a more conscious use of the trappings of Art Nouveau in the earlier work and a greater range of colour in the later. But it is remarkable how consistent Rackham was and, consequently, how difficult it is sometimes to date his work. He was the one illustrator to ride the Depression of the 1930s, and the general indifference to the work of the great illustrators that continued up to the time of World War II. Without doubt he was the greatest children's illustrator of the twentieth century, and the Gift books he produced were the nucleus around which the so-called Golden Age of British book illustration developed.

The snakes and ladders of foliage and bubbles were only one aspect of Art Nouveau. Equally important was the eccentric balancing of masses that was derived from Japanese art. It was this feature that gave the illustrations of Jessie Wilcox Smith, in the United States, such individuality. She applied these daring new concepts of perspective to the picturing of the domestic interiors of twentieth-century America. She interpreted reality with imagination, and was unparalleled as an observer of children, their habits and their postures. Her illustrations tended to lay stress on the bond between mother and child. The figures bordered on the sentimental with the children invariably clean and lovable, the mothers beautiful to look at, capable of infinite tenderness and with hands unsullied by housework. It was dangerously near to chocolate-box art, but the structure of the pictures was often subtle and effective. She made the space between the figures come alive, so that even when, in the picture of a child, the mother was not shown, one knew that if the picture had been extended she would be there, immaculate and adoring.

The same type of structure, based on unusual shapes and angles, was also used by the Australian artist Edith Alsop in 1910 for an illustration, 'Across the shining sands we fly' (C28) in the book *Some Australian Children's Songs* which her sister, Marion Alsop, had composed to poems by Dorothy Frances McCrae. The diagonal placing of the children, with the figure of the front girl cut off by the edge of the page, helped to emphasize the feeling of movement. The windswept hair of the group, and the modelling of the clothes of the little girl in the rear as she fights her way across the sand, rubbing the grit from her eyes, added to this effect. And in the distance, as if in homage to the great source of her inspiration, Edith Alsop shyly introduced a dotted version of Hokusai's wave.

Dots, for decoration and suggestion, were one of the Beardsleyan legacies, and Jessie M. King, a product of the Glasgow School of Art, with its individual interpretation of Art Nouveau, mixed these with equally archetypal memories of a Celtic past. Although virtually all her art, in a long working life, related to children, very few of the books she illustrated were specifically intended for the nursery. She created a gossamer world of slender maidens, whose full skirts had dewdrops for beading and garlands of flowers for braiding. As remote from time and reality as Maeterlinck's Melisande, her damsels trod lightly over meadows covered with tiny flowers without crushing a single one underfoot. One drawing of hers in *Littledom Castle* of 1903, a splendid compendium of fairy stories illustrated by various artists, Rackham and Hugh Thomson amongst them, sums up her art (103). Like the fairy's wand in the picture, it spoke of magic and wonder, and always left behind a trail of flowers and sparkling things. Jessie M. King's was an enchanted vision and could only be found between the covers of fairy books. Jessie Wilcox Smith's inspiration, on the other hand, was naturalistic, and belonged to the real world outside. What the two artists had in common was a genuine love for the child and an ability to convey, each in her own way, a reassurance that no harm would befall him.

Many of Jessie M. King's actual pictures, as well as the one wallpaper she designed – a delicate interpretation of 'Sing a Song of Sixpence', which was manufactured in 1906, had nursery themes. She drew several series of pictures intended for the nursery: one of 'Days', beginning with 'Monday's Child', and one of 'Months', beginning with 'January brings the Snow'. For *The Studio* magazine she did two exquisite series: 'Seven Happy Days', with quotations from John Davidson and other poets, and 'Good King Wenceslas', in which she used the text of the carol as a starting point for a departure into her own dream world. A number of her illustrations for fairy tales – 'The Little Mermaid', 'The Six Swans', 'Rapunzel' and 'The Sleeping Beauty' – although completed as watercolour drawings, were possibly done for exhibition and never intended for publication in book form (C29). Her drawings made an original contribution to Art Nouveau, both in her use of wispy curves of line and in her way of incorporating the title written in her own individual style, with each letter separated from its neighbours by a tiny star or dot for, like her fellow artists of the Glasgow School, she looked upon captions as an integral part of the design.

Jessie M. King painted plates and mugs with children and rabbits at play in a landscape of flowers, and a splendid Ali Baba vase with all forty thieves painted on the outside. One outstanding ceramic work was a plaque of nine tiles making up the nursery rhyme 'Ride-a-cock-horse', which she did purely as an exercise in design. She made dolls' houses and dolls' furniture, and wrote two books: *The Little Town of Never Weary* and *How Cinderella was able to go to the Ball*, to show children how to make these toys and print fabric in batik patterns.

The most ambitious designs she executed were those for a real nursery that was exhibited at an exhibition of nursery design at the Musée Galliera in Paris in 1912. The furnishing of the room was complete down to the

150 Jessie M. King: rocking-horse, 'Brightling', painted wood, 1912.

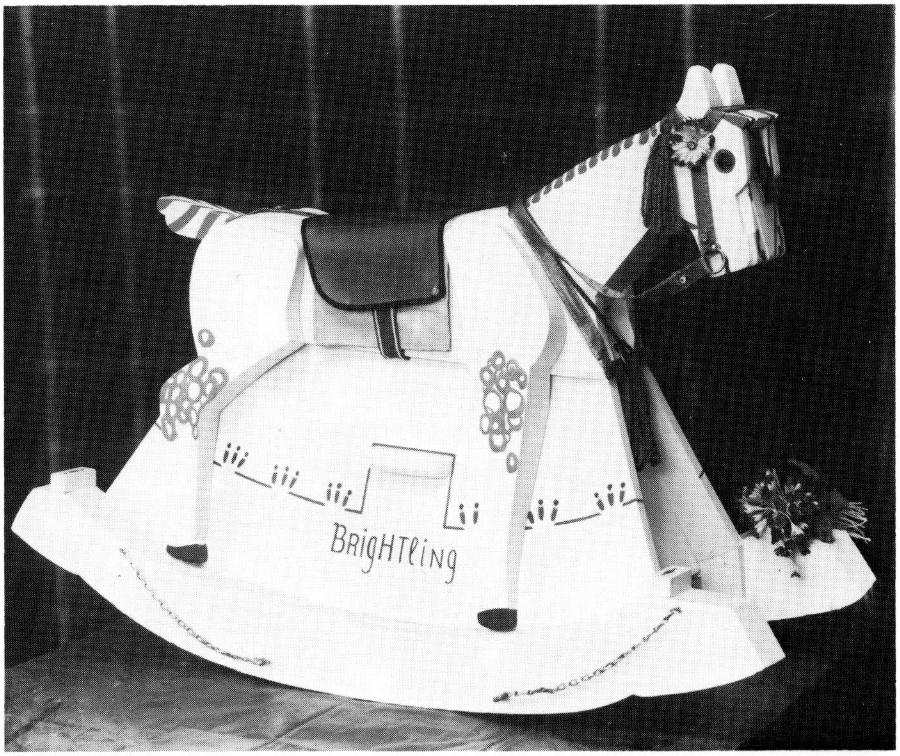

151 Jessie M. King: nursery designed for exhibition at the Musée Galliera, Paris, 1912.

murals, the stained glass panels for the windows, and the toys, which included the most playfully extrovert rocking-horse ever seen (150). The furniture itself was simple, with verticals and horizontals stressed at the expense of the curve, in the style that Charles Rennie Mackintosh had brought to such refinement. Painted white it was perhaps a little stark, but it was attractive, modern looking, and perfectly suited to the needs of the nursery (151).

As Jessie M. King's art progressed, her colour remained subtle but the swirls of fine lines, that she always drew on vellum with the finest of nibs, became more angular and her figures more awkward, as if she was consciously trying to renounce her Art Nouveau past. Her introduction to the art of batik had brought an interest in flat areas of colour and a stencil-like technique that broke up the flow of her forms. Her style seemed more earthbound and, although still recognizably her own, began to relate more to the 'thirties art of Gladys Peto and Phyllis Cooper, and the full gowns that her maidens wore in the earlier illustrations came to be replaced by more clinging up-to-date styles.

Annie French, who followed Jessie M. King at the Glasgow School of Art, worked in a related style but was far less prolific an artist. Like Jessie M. King's, her girls were enveloped in voluminous gowns, speckled, as indeed was the whole surface of her pictures, with flowers and jewels that were almost pointillistic in their profusion (C30). Her subjects too were of the fairy world, but a part that was more arcane than Jessie M. King's. There was something a little sinister about her characters. The thoughts that lay unspoken in their minds were those of the mysteries of forests and spells. Their magic dealt with transformation, not of creation.

Although Annie French painted pictures for the nursery she never attempted to illustrate nursery books. Her decorative style, though, was ideally suited to the many picture postcards, often enriched with metallic paints, that she was commissioned to design for an age when the postcard was not only a vehicle for communication but an art form in its own right. Before 1900, most of the coloured greetings cards in Britain and America had been printed by chromolithography and, like the pictures produced for children's books or for framing, were printed by continental firms or their subsidiaries in Great Britain. The revolution in colour printing at the turn of the century extended to greetings cards, and printers seized on the opportunities that half-tone photography offered to manufacture bright and attractive cards relatively cheaply.

Picture postcard manufacturers were eager to introduce novelties for what had quickly become a collecting craze. Many cards were published illustrating children or nursery subjects, either for actual use by children or because, like many of today's greetings cards, it was considered astute marketing to issue cards with children on the front. Individual cards showing babies in action had been manufactured for many years (152)

C28 (opposite) Edith Alsopp: 'Across the Shining Sands We Fly' from *Some Australian Children's Songs* by Dorothy Frances Macrae, George Robertson & Co., Melbourne, 1910.

C29 (overleaf) Jessie M. King: *The Sleeping Beauty*, pen, ink and watercolour on vellum, 13 in. × 18½ in., *c.* 1924. Private collection.

but, from 1903 onwards, publishers were anxious to obtain exclusive rights for designs by popular children's illustrators, and cards of Golliwogg, Buster Brown and Teddy Bear were issued.

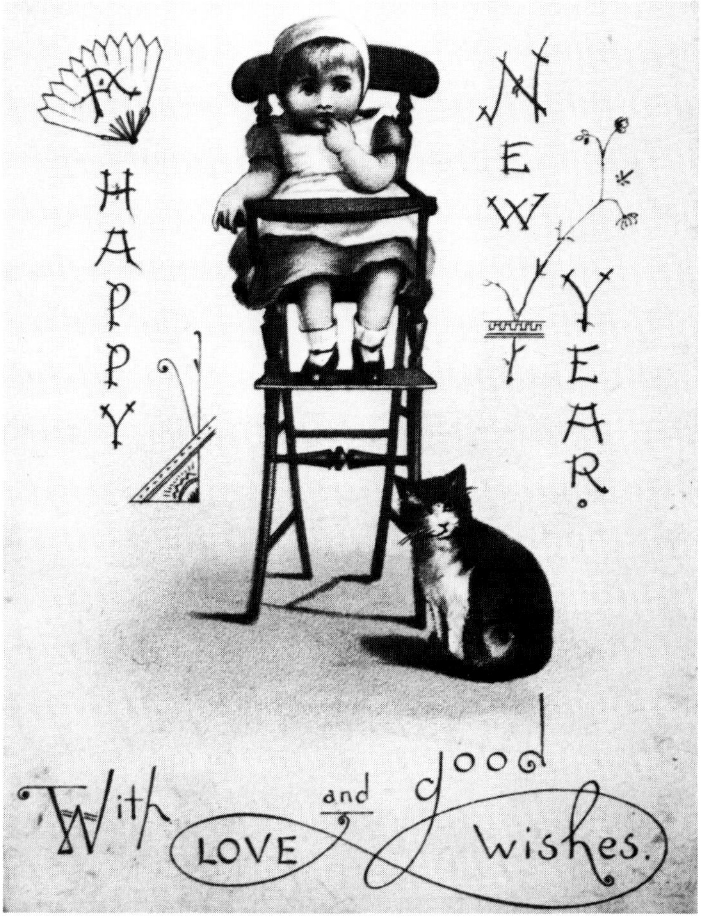

152 Nursery greetings card: 'Happy New Year', 1890. Museum of Childhood, Edinburgh.

Many specialist greetings card or art-publishing firms: Tuck's, Valentine's and Medici in Great Britain, or Ullman's or Reinthal and Newman's in the United States, manufactured nursery cards. Some cards, like the many humorous ones designed by Mabel Lucie Attwell, were available singly; others were sold in packets of six or twelve with different designs on the same theme. Flower Fairies, Jewel Fairies, The Months, Scenes from Fairy Tales or Nursery Rhymes, were all to be found as sets of nursery postcards. Some of the book publishing companies issued cards reproducing illustrations taken from their own books. Warne's brought out several series of cards featuring Randolph Caldecott's nursery rhyme illustrations, and A. and C. Black's issued cards illustrated by Charles Folkard and Ida Rentoul Outhwaite, with whom they had contracts.

JESSIE M. KING

ANNIE FREN
To Lydia from Annie, Christmas 1925

Novelty cards were also produced in which, like the Trick books, by pulling a tab, Cinderella could be transformed, in an instant, from her rags by the fireside to her splendour at the ball.

c30 Annie French: *A Fairy Tale*, pen, ink and watercolour, $8\frac{1}{2}$ in. × 10 in. Private collection.

153a (left) Nursery postcard: 'Girls and Boys Come Out to Play' by Dorothy M. Wheeler, A. & C. Black, 1936.

153b (above) Nursery postcard: 'Merry Makers', Edward Gros Co. Inc., New York, *c.* 1900.

154a (far left) Nursery postcard: 'The House that Jack Built' by Randolph Caldecott, Frederick Warne & Co. Ltd., 1916.

154b (left) Nursery postcard: 'The Nursery' series by Henriette Willebeek le Mair, Erwen Thomas, Amsterdam, 1917.

Original work for nursery postcards was commissioned from illustrators, both celebrated and unknown. Cecily Barker, who specialized in the Flower Fairies; John Hassall; Tom Brown, who had illustrated in many of the early comic papers; Jessie M. King; Rie Cramer, who, like Molly

Brett, created her own playland of happy little betrousered animals; Joyce Mercer and Phyllis Cooper, all designed many beautiful sets of nursery postcards in Britain. Cards were produced by firms not usually associated with the trade. Advertising postcards with, for example, 'The Campbell Kids', were common, and Augener, the music publishers, issued a number of sets with designs, pale, low-keyed and almost Japanese in their delicacy, by the Dutch artist Henriette Wilbeek le Maire (153a, b), (154a, b).

Many of the British manufacturers had offices in the United States, and both they and the local publishers commissioned cards from well-known American illustrators. 'The Sunbonnet Babies', drawn first by Bertha L. Corbett and later by Bernhardt Wall (155), as well as Rose O'Neill's 'Kewpies' appeared in this way.

People all over the world collected postcards, and the number of post-card albums now to be found in junk shops point to the popularity of the hobby in its day. In the United States the craze died down around the time of World War I, but the manufacture of picture postcards, including nursery cards, continued in Great Britain and on the Continent. In recent times postcard collecting has returned as a hobby and as an investment, and older nursery cards now enjoy a recognition greater than when they first appeared. Like the Gift books they have become too precious to be entrusted to children, and the choice Mable Lucie Attwell or Annie French cards are now put safely away in adults' albums, well out of the reach of eager jammy fingers.

155 Nursery postcard: 'April', from *The Sunbonnet Babies – the Months* by Bernhardt Wall, Ullman Mfg. Co., USA, 1905.

CHAPTER II

Gift Books and Cuteness

The modern Gift book was largely a British phenomenon. It occupied the talents of the best book illustrators in the country for almost twenty years, and was the outcome of Carl Hentschell's new photographic process which permitted, for the first time, an accurate reproduction of colour work. The process allowed artists greater freedom in their illustrations, but redirected their thinking from linear to tonal values, with richness replacing clarity. It both inspired illustrators and corrupted them.

Between 1905, when the first of the modern Gift books, Arthur Rackham's *Rip Van Winkle*, was published, and World War I, which marked the beginning of their decline, the major publishing houses, each with its own group of illustrators, vied with one another to capture the Christmas market in luxury children's books. Publishers sang their siren songs to the adults who were their potential purchasers, and the adult conception of what a special book for a child should look like determined the year's offerings. Something out of the ordinary was needed for a Christmas gift, and costly books, larger, thicker and more splendidly bound than usual, with specially commissioned illustrations printed by the new colour process, were published by each house. Their splendour was self-defeating. The volumes were works of art in themselves, and had a sophistication that no child could be expected to appreciate. Perhaps, in the spirit of the very first Gift books (those of the 1830s), the proper recipient of these de luxe editions should have been the sweetheart rather than the child. They were, in fact, considered too good for children.

The illustrations in the Gift books were almost aways reproductions of watercolours. They made full use of the new process and were printed on heavy art paper and individually mounted. Publishers rivalled one another to produce ever more sumptuous examples of their artists' work. Hodder's had the most extensive list of illustrators, with Dulac, Detmold, Hugh Thomson and Nielsen. Heinemann's, however, had Arthur Rackham. All the Gift book illustrators, each in his own way, produced work of a splendour that had not been seen before in children's books. If Rackham's work revealed a supreme sensitivity in the grading of olive and sepia tints, Nielsen's was like the sudden opening of a casket of precious stones. If Heath Robinson achieved an almost Renoir-like effect in his experiments on the subtleties of light and shade, Dulac was the master of invention and of the decorative possibilities of colour.

156 Paul Woodroffe: *Nursery Songs*, T.C. & E.C. Jack, 1907.

The works chosen to display these talents were invariably those of fantasy, and fairy tales provided the best examples. Inevitably there was much duplication of titles during the reign of the Gift books. Rackham and Nielsen both illustrated *Grimm*; Dulac, Detmold and Virginia Sterrett (an artist unusual in Gift book work being both American and female), all illustrated an *Arabian Nights*; Dulac and Sterrett both gave their different interpretations of *Tanglewood Tales* as well as illustrating some of the French fairy tales of the Comtesse de Segur; and Harry Clarke, Heath Robinson and almost everybody else illustrated an *Andersen* (C31).

The standard was high, and each chosen illustrator brought his own personal vision to the interpretation of the text. If the books were often barred from the nursery itself, even where they were nursery orientated, children were at least allowed to see them under supervision. If their very awesomeness made them special, the memories of those books, in the children who grew up with them in the home, will have been very special ones.

When the Great War came it brought with it a deep and often agonizing reappraisal of priorities in which Gift books were not of the highest importance. By the end of the war the Age of Certainty had vanished. Reality no longer had the softness of watercolour, but was hard-edged, angular and bright, both to look at and to listen to. Throughout the world the tendrils of Art Nouveau were dying, and when the shrivelled twigs were examined they were seen to have formed themselves into the more geometric shapes of Art Deco.

The decline of the Gift book showed that growing alongside, but quite overshadowed by them, had been many less pretentious, but no less worthy examples of illustrated books for the nursery. Paul Woodroffe's *Nursery Songs* of 1907 were drawn with a beauty and precision worthy of a Book of Hours (156). Hilda Broughton's illustration 'Mary Rides', from Lady Bell's *Singing Circle* of 1911 was a fine example of modern genre composition using vignettes of contemporary forms of transport as decoration (157).

It was in this often more popular field of profane art for the nursery that the conflict with the more esoteric world of the Gift books was most apparent. The gaudy reproductions of jolly boys and girls building sandcastles were good salesmanship but poor art. They offered merely the themes without the variations, but children loved them. Artistic subtlety is lost on children and is sometimes destructive to appreciation. Art for the nursery can never be solely the art of suggestion but must always contain the art of statement. It was in this way, by inviting appreciation at more than one level, that the art of Mabel Lucie Attwell became so popular in the nursery.

The 'Kiddiwinks' and the 'Diddums', as Mabel Lucie Attwell called her little children, owed much, in their simple bold outlines, to the work

157 Hilda Broughton: 'Mary Rides' from *The Singing Circle* by Lady Florence Bell, Longmans Green & Co., 1911.

MABEL
LUCIE
ATTWELL

of her teacher John Hassall. The Mabel Lucie Attwell baby was invariably solid, without visible wrists, ankles or neck. The feet were always firmly set on the ground, the strap-over shoes taut and unyielding, the ankle-length socks in wrinkles, and the little skirt or trousers bulging over a large tummy, as if nappies were still being worn. The features were subtly placed dots, with tiny mouths nestling between chubby rosy cheeks. If a finger was not being sucked a tear was falling, and a doll was either being clutched or was within gathering distance (158). Even the familiar signature had a dumpiness that was unexpected from a person of Mabel Lucie Attwell's tall slender build. The Mabel Lucie Attwell baby was, in fact, one of the first arrivals in the nursery to show 'cuteness'.

Cuteness is the active form of sentimentality and is generally a phenomenon of the young – Jiminy Cricket was one of the few cute 'Oldies'. It is basically a plea for admiration or endearment by display of those qualities of brightness, freshness, intelligence or precociousness, that helps to remove the barriers of reserve that a person sets up at the initial stages of social contact. It is brasher and harder than coquetry, to which it is related. It employs trigger signs designed to expedite the establishment of rapport: the rolling eye, the mannered expressions, the angular postures and the artificial vivacity (C32), (159). It uses exaggerations of gesture, dress and speech to express these pleas; so clothing may be too large, as in 'Yankee Doodle' or Walt Disney's 'Dopey', or too small, as with the 'Kiddiwinks'. Verbally it uses a language, either more sophisticated or, paradoxically, more babyish, than that character should be able to command. It incorporates mis-applications of speech, as when a Mabel Lucie Attwell baby says 'I'se got boo eyes ...'. The character – and this is as true of Rose O'Neill's 'Kewpies', those cupid-like people with the top knots, that were an amalgam of the 'Brownies' and the putti of heavenly choirs (160); of Will Owen's 'Bisto Kids' and Grace Drayton's 'Campbell Kids', as of anything in Disney – has become over-assertive. An untruthfulness has crept in, together with a rather dangerous parody of aspects of life that would otherwise never have merited consideration. Communication such as this is more fundamental than words, and plumbs hidden depths of our personalities in mysterious and disconcerting ways. The ability of children of nursery age to harness such instinctive knowledge and power is awesome to behold, and adds weight to the hypothesis that our bodies are no more than vehicles for selfish genes striving for immortality with subtlety and invidiousness.

Cuteness is successful because the signals are attractive and easily understood. The visual elements far outweigh the auditory ones, and blend readily with other forms of stylization because all of them belong to a common elemental pool. This is why cuteness in animated cartoons, which are the epitome of visual shorthand, is so easy to achieve. The nursery wall picture of Bo-Peep makes an ideal decoration because it is

158 (opposite) Mabel Lucie Attwell: 'Have you ever been caught by the Fairies?', from *Princess Marie-José's Children's Book*, Cassell & Co., 1916. © Lucie Attwell Ltd.

159 Grace Drayton: 'The Campbell Kids', 1927 version.

160 Rose O'Neill: the Kewpie doll, *c.* 1935, celluloid. Museum of Childhood, Edinburgh.

C31 Virginia Sterrett: 'They were three months passing through the forest', from *Old French Fairy Tales*, The Penn Publishing Co., Philadelphia, 1920.

entirely composed of emotive symbols (C33). The cuteness of the figure of Bo-Peep herself, with the teardrop on her cheek, her finger at her lips, partly to be bitten in anguish and partly to silence the little animals who have come to help find her sheep, blends perfectly with the assemblage of the stock props of an idyllic landscape. The picture is unified by the unyielding pen outline given to each of the components, by the bright, largely flat colours, and by the compression of the scene to fit a frame, all of which points to the animated cartoon as the source of inspiration. It is an ideal nursery image because it offers immediate recognition of scene, character and situation. It is superficial art because it tells nothing about that character beyond the moment it has captured. It is utterly delightful because it is such a blatant seduction.

Mabel Lucie Attwell did not live in a cultural vacuum. She must have been aware that a vogue already existed in the United States for the 'Campbell Kids' that Grace Drayton had created in 1905 as an advertisement for Campbell's Soups (159). Equally popular were the 'Sunbonnet Babies' that Bertha L. Corbett, yet another of Howard Pyle's pupils, had first illustrated in 1902 in an attempt to prove that a figure could be made expressive even when the face was hidden (155), (161). This was a principle held also by Edward Ardizzone, who always maintained that the most interesting drawing of a child was from behind (162).

68 The Sunbonnet Babies' Primer
"Ring around the roses."
"Ring around the roses,
A pot full of posies.
The one who stoops last
Shall tell whom she loves best."

161 Bertha Corbett Melcher: illustration for *The Sunbonnet Babies' Primer* by Eulalie Osgood Grover, Minneapolis, 1900.

The new chunky breed of children – Grace Drayton's 'Dolly Dimples', 'Toodley' and the 'Campbell Kids'; the 'Sunbonnet Babies' and their straw-hatted male equivalents 'The Overall Boys' – caught on in America. They were made as cuddly dolls and appeared in many forms in the nursery, from handkerchiefs and feeders to money boxes and expensive silver christening presents from Tiffany's.

Mabel Lucie Attwell used a similar shape for the babies she drew and, by giving them a variety of appealing facial expressions produced an image that was to become the most famous depiction of childhood in the twentieth century. The Mabel Lucie Attwell child is still a recognized symbol. It has been featured on postcards, toys, plaques for the bathroom or kitchen, on tins of biscuits, soap, clothing, wallpaper and on posters for sponsors as diverse as the London Underground and music-hall conjuring acts (28). Mabel Lucie Attwell dolls, both boy and girl, and the innumerable books she illustrated have graced most nurseries during the last three-quarters of a century. Jessie Wilcox Smith illustrated the ideal form of a child seen through the eyes of the mother. Mabel Lucie Attwell's children were imagined, if not through the eyes of the child, then at least in the way that adults felt that children saw themselves.

It was Jessie Wilcox Smith, though, who first clothed her children in what one would now call modern dress. For the first time in illustration children became individuals and no longer the doll-like toddlers who were commonly found in nursery books. The free, loosely-fitting, short clothes,

VIRGINIA STERRETT

Frances Brundage

ankle-length socks and shoes with simple overstraps that her children were shown wearing belonged to the twentieth century and influenced fashion as much as Kate Greenaway's had done. Because of her work, the very manner in which children were illustrated came to be revised in both Britain and America. But it was the Mabel Lucie Attwell child that made the greater impact. Jessie Wilcox Smith's children belonged to their time and, as fashions and taste changed, so they were left behind. The neutral children were forgotten. The impact made by the cute was remembered. Mabel Lucie Attwell's children belonged to the world of hyper-reality and make-believe and so became immortal.

C32 Frances Brundage: 'Petruchio and Katherine', from *The Children's Shakespeare*, Raphael Tuck & Sons Ltd., London & New York, *c.* 1890. Chromolithograph.

162 Edward Ardizzone: 'Henry and Mary' (detail) from *The Penny Fiddle* by Robert Graves, Cassell & Co., 1960. Private collection.

CHAPTER 12

The Rise of the Picture Book

Ernest Shepard's first book for children, an edition of *Tom Brown's Schooldays*, was illustrated in 1905. The first of the Pooh books, *When We Were Very Young*, did not appear until almost twenty years later, in 1924. It told of the adventures of Christopher Robin Milne and his real life toys, Pooh, Eyore, Kanga, Piglet and Tigger, and marked the beginning of a collaboration between A.A. Milne and Shepard that was to ensure immortality for both the author and the artist (C34).

Parodied and often derided for their precious bourgeois values, *When We Were Very Young* and its three sequels, *Winnie the Pooh* of 1926, *Now We Are Six* of 1927 and *The House at Pooh Corner* of 1928, have outlasted all their detractors. Pooh himself, although he never smiled, and was never very young, immediately became a nursery favourite, to be loved alongside Peter Rabbit and Teddy.

Ernest Shepard was one of the few illustrators - Hugh Thomson, Charles Brock and Edward Ardizzone were others - who could bring life to a face by the careful placing of a dot for the eyes and nose, and the tiniest line for the mouth. His drawings are totally convincing, and he leaves us in no doubt that this is the way that a little boy comes downstairs, or kicks his way through autumn leaves, or gets dressed (163).

Middle-class families appreciated the wry, yet dignified, humour of these small volumes as documents of reassurance that the values of what seemed like a vanished age were not altogether lost. The relative sobriety of the presentation of the books themselves offered an old-fashioned sense of familiarity in the 1920s when the Gift book had been replaced in Britain by the 'Annual', the 'Bumper Book' and the 'Compendium', all of which were easier to compile and cheaper to produce than Gift books. The post-war nursery books attracted new publishers, and artists who could provide livelier, if more ephemeral work than the Gift book illustrators were suddenly in demand.

The new artists depicted the nursery as a world of balloons and tea parties, of Pierrots, clowns and Chinese lanterns. There was a greater freedom of dress and manners. It was a noisier, more boisterous world than before the war, and the illustrators pictured it accordingly. The rows of dots that had tattooed the illustrations of Aubrey Beardsley, and the trail of stardust and petals that had followed Jessie M. King's girls, were transformed into a multitude of bubbles that floated about the large satin bows in the bobbed hair of the new, thoroughly modern little girls (164). Phyllis Cooper, in the annual *My Favourite* of 1928, illustrated a poem, 'How we acted Charades', with slippered children, short-haired and short-skirted, leaping around to exuberant 'Hurrays' amid a tumbling cascade of party balloons. Gladys Peto, in a nursery wall picture of the same period, used similar motifs in sheer enjoyment of their potential as pattern (165). Although expressed in a more earthbound manner, something of the spirit of Kay Nielsen in his *In Powder and Crinoline* of 1913 persisted in the memories of festoons and garlands, pom-poms and streamers, but the world it pictured was no longer one of dreams and eternity;

US TWO

Wherever I am, there's always Pooh,
There's always Pooh and Me.
Whatever I do, he wants to do,
" Where are you going to-day ? " says Pooh :
" Well, that's very odd 'cos I was too.
Let's go together," says Pooh, says he.
" Let's go together," says Pooh.

163 Ernest Shepard: 'Us Two' from *Now We Are Six* by A.A. Milne, Methuen & Co. Ltd., 1927. Line illustration by E.H. Shepard © under the Berne Convention. Reproduced by permission of Curtis Brown Ltd., London, Methuen & Co. Ltd., and E.P. Dutton Inc., New York.

164 Phyllis Cooper: 'War and Peace' from *My Favourites*, R. Tuck & Sons Ltd., 1928.

165 Nursery picture: *First Steps* by Gladys Peto, pen, ink and watercolour, *c.* 1929.

it was one of reality and immediacy. The fairy tale was now lit with fairy lights, for this was the age of electricity, and the Beardsleyan candles had all melted away.

It was only a short step, with one foot in the world of Art Nouveau and the other searching beyond, to risk all and enter the new world of Art Deco. In 1928, Joyce Mercer, in 'A Surprise for Cathy', was drawing the fashionable bubbles and wavy lines that belonged to the contemporary manner of decorating children's books. Within the drawing, however, could be seen the stylization that foreshadowed the harlequinized cubism of her later work for the annuals and nursery postcards she designed in the years immediately preceding World War II (166).

Children's annuals, like fairies, were never as popular in the United States as in Great Britain. Closest to them, perhaps, were the collections of picture stories of magazine favourites such as the Brownies, Gelett Burgess's 'Goops' or Buster Brown. The reason was partly a shortage of characters known on a national scale, there being no nationwide distribution of a particular newspaper with its comic section, although syndication of a series helped to overcome this. More important, though, was

166 Joyce Mercer: 'A Surprise for Cathy' from *My Favourite*, R. Tuck & Sons Ltd., 1928.

OBEDIENCE
THE Goops are very hard to kill,
So they hang out the Window-sill;
Down the Banisters they slide—
I could do it if I tried;
But when Mother tells me "don't,"
Then, of course
I really won't!

167 Gelett Burgess: 'Obedience' from *Goops and How to Be Them*, Frederick A. Stokes Co., 1900.

the early awakening in the United States, long before it happened in Great Britain, of a sense of responsibility towards children's books by the various Libraries Associations. A number of educationalist groups, concerned about the quality of the children's books that were being published, sought to promote books that were inexpensive, well printed, entertaining and, if possible, educational. They wished to recapture the simplicity and integrity of the old Toy books. The result was the 'Picture' book, and a new age of the artist-author: the creator who conceived books in visual rather than literary terms.

Ever since the introduction into the West of Japanese prints, one of the aims of graphic artists had been to escape from the tyranny imposed by the rectangular page on its text or its illustrations. In Crane's Toy books the rigidity of the typeface was deliberately disrupted by Crane using his own handwriting to fragment the text, much as William Blake had done long before in his *Songs of Innocence*. Howard Pyle had been very concerned about page decoration and had experimented with unusual forms in *Pepper and Salt* and in some of the poems he illustrated for children's magazines. Gelett Burgess, in 1900, achieved in his 'Goops' books an even more modern effect by abolishing borders altogether and allowing the shape of the print on the page to be determined by the lengths of the lines of verse and the placing of the decorations (167).

Art Nouveau illustrators in general had disliked the rectangular border but, although disrupting it, they still tended to enclose the text within boundaries of their own devising. One of the first nursery artists to reverse the normal process and allow the text of each page of a book to make inroads into the illustrations, had been Boutet de Monvel. In his *Jeanne d'Arc* he had made enclaves of text within the pictures and had shaped his illustrations to interlock with blocks of the narrative. He had used double-page spreads, and had made single pictures step outside their frames in an attempt to achieve continuity. Other artists used pictorial techniques to break down the rigid divisions between a block of text and its illustration. The American, E. Boyd Smith, in his *Chicken World* of 1910, had given his illustrations exceptionally wide borders which he had then proceeded to fill with alternative scenes of the story. Heath Robinson, in *Uncle Lubin* had used the margins on the page of text to take drawings which showed the prelude to, or the consequence of, the main illustration on the opposite page (145).

Devices such as these formed the basis of the new American Picture books where they were used to give equal importance to the text and the illustrations. They tried to establish a feeling of movement that would encourage the child to read on and turn the page. Wanda Gág's *Millions of Cats*, published in 1928, was one of the first to do so. The actual shape of the pictures was made to relate to a particular episode in the story of the little old man who set out one day to find a cat that would be a companion for his wife and himself in their loneliness. Wanda Gág played games with clouds in her pictures, setting them as cottage-loaf lumps, drawn in perspective, like stepping-stones for the reader to move along and arrive at whatever the artist wished to emphasize. Even more effectively, she aligned the ever-increasing number of cats in such a way that the reader had to follow the procession through to the end, and so weave his way through the whole picture (168). This freedom of movement was matched by the cursive lettering that was deliberately designed to help the flow of the book, much as Walter Crane's Roman lettering had matched his more classical pictures. Gelett Burgess had let the space flow round each drawing; Wanda Gág went further and consciously manipulated the free space as if it were malleable and plastic, to give unity to the whole book. Picture books were created, not compiled. From the beginning, their bright format, made possible by the newest and most versatile method of printing by offset-lithography, and the use of themes pertinent to the daily life of the child, helped it to flourish in America under the admiring approval of educationalists.

The new books were meant to be used rather than treasured, and were never conceived as being other than ephemeral. The genre was sufficiently comprehensive to accommodate a wide range of styles. Lois Lenski, in her books illustrating the life of the 'Small' and 'Little' families, took simplicity to extremes with an economy of line that previously only Burgess had attempted (169). She tried to show the interaction between the child and the seemingly trivial happenings of everyday life. She had the ability to see with the eyes of a child the magic of Mummy baking, or the sheer bliss of Daddy shaving. Using merely a circle for the heads, and simple outlines for the bodies, she related to the child his own world in child-sized terms.

168 Wanda Gág: illustration and accompanying text from *Millions of Cats*, by Wanda Gág, © 1928 by Coward-McCann Inc.; copyright renewed © 1956 by Robert Janssen; used by permission of Coward-McCann Inc.

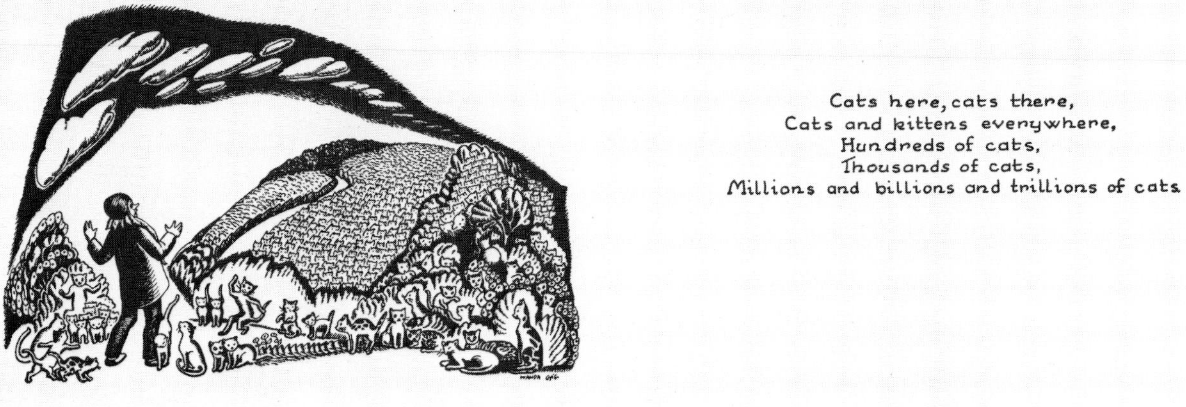

Cats here, cats there,
Cats and kittens everywhere,
Hundreds of cats,
Thousands of cats,
Millions and billions and trillions of cats.

169 Lois Lenski: illustration from *Papa Small*, Oxford University Press, 1951. © Lois Lenski/David Mackay Inc., USA.

170 Robert Lawson: illustration from *The Story of Ferdinand* by Monro Leaf. Illustration © 1936 by Robert Lawson. © renewed 1955 by John W. Boyd. Reprinted by permission of Viking Penguin Inc.

Robert Lawson who, in 1936, illustrated Munro Leaf's *The Story of Ferdinand*, the bull who wouldn't fight, used black and white as concentrated colour to picture the contrast between the dazzling sunlight and deep shadows of Spain. Most of the Picture book artists wrote and illustrated their own work. Lawson showed that it was possible for an author and an artist to collaborate within the new idiom to produce a work that was unified in thought and feeling, in both story and illustration (170).

The illustration of the Picture books served the very opposite function of the *hors texte* plates of the Gift books. Its purpose was to allow the child to take in the picture and the story simultaneously rather than pause and contemplate the picture in the old way and interrupt the flow. Many of the Picture books, in trying to be true to life, tended to become didactic but, unlike the books of the previous century, they tried to explain to the child and teach by guidance instead of intimidation. Beneath their apparent directness, however, they could often be subtly and unintentionally deceptive, just as everything that is selective deceives in some way. The child they presented, like his Victorian forerunners, was idealized, sterile and free from natural clutter, dirt or emotion. The need for made-up stories was too great, and the neo-didacts ultimately had to capitulate to the taste of the readers. The medium was ideal but the message had to change, and it was a Frenchman who showed how the adjustment could be made.

In Babar the elephant, Jean de Brunhof created a wise and lovable hero whose struggle and ultimate victory was the stuff of success for a book. *The Story of Babar*, in 1931, was the first of a number of books of Babar's

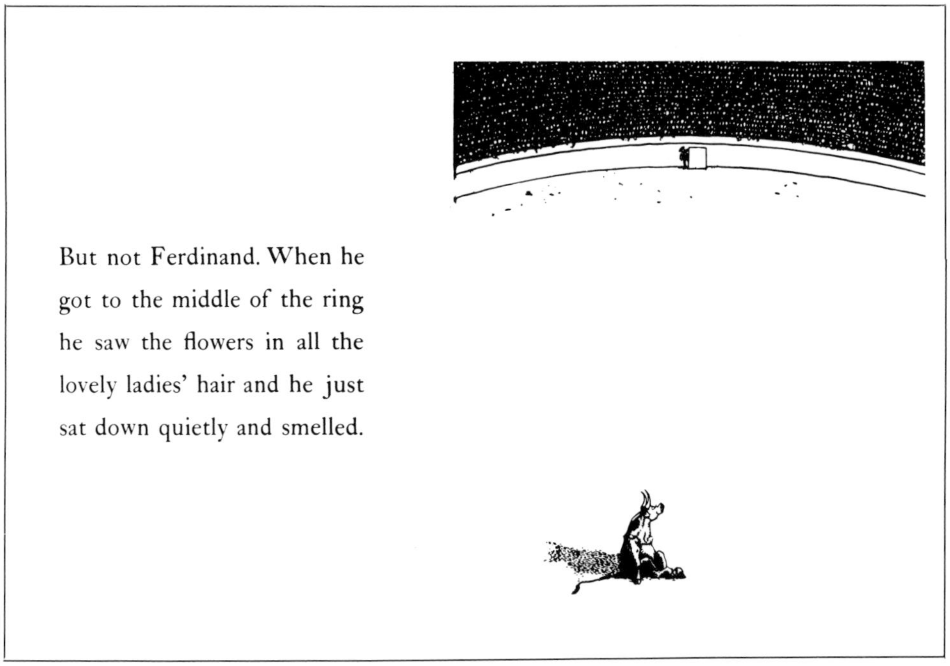
But not Ferdinand. When he got to the middle of the ring he saw the flowers in all the lovely ladies' hair and he just sat down quietly and smelled.

Babar was so pleased
with his purchases,
and satisfied
with his appearance
that he paid a visit
to the photographer.

171 Jean de Brunhof: illustration from *The Story of Babar*, Librairie Hachette, Paris, 1931; © 1933, renewed 1961 by Random House Inc. and reprinted by permission of Random House Inc. and Methuen and Co. Ltd.

adventures: a series that was continued after the author's early death in 1937 by his son Laurent. Jean de Brunhof was, by profession, a painter, and *The Story of Babar* was of the true nature of Picture books, with a careful balance between the simple direct pictures and the hand-written text. In each story Babar was given sufficient human attributes to involve the child reader so that, as King of the Elephants, he was made to wear a crown, sit on a throne, sleep in a bed and drive around in a motor car. Underneath this façade, de Brunhof used the story as a polemic to express his love for living creatures and declare his own hopes for the ideals of Western civilization at a difficult time in its history (171).

The Picture books did not cause a revolution in children's publishing. In both Britain and the United States their acceptance was gradual and many splendid nursery books in the traditional forms continued to be produced. Lawson Wood, one of the early members of the London Sketch Club, illustrated many books between the wars and, in his *Nursery Rhyme Book* of 1933, the emblematic coloured pictures with their flat patterns and idiosyncratic perspective, printed by half-tone photography, were as vivid as any produced by the newer lithographic process (C35). In the United States, Lancing Campbell's illustrations for the adventures of *Uncle Wiggily* and his friends rivalled in popularity those of Johnny Gruelle for his *Raggedy Ann* (135), (172).

British publishers, especially, favoured the 'star' system: a series of books relating the adventures of the same character. The star could be a favourite individual, such as Hugh Lofting's 'Doctor Dolittle', drawn in the author's Thurberesque manner; or George Studdy's zany Dalmatian dog 'Bonzo' (173). It could be a group of characters, such as the 'Bruin Boys', whom the children knew from their comics, or Rupert and his friends, from the *Daily Express*. The wireless also contributed, with Hulme Beaman's adventures of 'Larry the Lamb', 'Mr Growser' and their fellow citizens of 'Toytown' in the well-known children's programme. Most important of all, the star system tried to use the fame of Gift book illustrators such as Charles Folkard, Nielsen, Rackham and Dulac, to introduce new work in a cheaper format that did not always do the artists full justice.

It took longer for the Picture book to become established in Great Britain than in America because there was less pressing need for change. As a style it had been known in Britain for many years. As far back as 1887 Walter Crane had written and illustrated a little-known book *Mr Michael Mouse Unfolds his Tale*, in which the handwritten text and the spontaneous watercolours foreshadowed the Picture books. William Nicholson used a similarly integrated style in his *Clever Bill* of 1926, and the Helen Bannerman and Beatrix Potter books were evident precursors of the form. However, the abundance of 'annuals' and 'Bumper' books, the comic papers for all ages, and the small treats like the *Henny Penny* books that could be bought at the local newsagents for a child's Saturday pocket money, induced a complacency in publishers, illustrators and public alike.

The essence of the Picture book was that it was a complete story, not a compendium of tales and, Babar notwithstanding, its eventual acceptance in Great Britain was due almost entirely to the success of one book. Edward Ardizzone's *Little Tim and the Brave Sea Captain* was the first and, in Ardizzone's own opinion, the best of a long series of Picture books that related to the adventures of a small boy and his friends Lucy and

Ginger. Significantly the book was first published in the United States before it appeared in Great Britain. The original edition, in the true fashion of the Picture books, reproduced the text in script. Only after World War II, when a second edition was issued, was stock type used. The new edition added one feature that was to become characteristic of Ardizzone's work: his use of the speech balloon which, until then, had been the provenance of children's comics. Ardizzone made it an important feature of the book, and used it, not to repeat information that had already been given in the text, but always to illuminate a new facet of an encounter.

Ardizzone was one of Britain's greatest illustrators for children. His handwriting was as much a part of his books as his drawing, and the distinctive script on the spines, done because he was not able to do beautiful formal lettering, were pointers to the recognition of his books on booksellers' shelves. His range of subject matter was large. He could draw a world of contemporary suburban children: their short trousers below their knees, their socks round their ankles, and their heavy shoes graceless and practical. At the same time, with equal facility, he could recreate the charm and dignity of a bygone age. He seemed to prefer the styles and mannerisms of the child as a wartime evacuee, and it is possible that, in the years to come, Ardizzone's will be the art that reveals the true

172 Nursery mug: 'Uncle Wiggily', 1924, made by Fred A. Wisch Inc., Seebring Pottery, Chicago, for the makers of Ovaltine.

173 G.E. Studdy: 'Bonzo', c. 1937.

essence of the 'forties. One might regret that there was no Ardizzone nursery wallpaper or curtain fabric, or that the only china he decorated was for adult use, but one is consoled by the fact that, had this not been so, there might have been fewer of his irreplaceable books.

In 1937, a year after the first *Tim* book was published, Kathleen Hale's *Orlando the Marmalade Cat* made its appearance. Less profound and sympathetic an animal than Babar, but more colourful and exciting, Orlando was manic and highly strung. Babar, as befitted his size and dignity, was a static creature. Orlando was ready to spring into action at the slightest excuse. Kathleen Hale's handwriting, like Ardizzone's, was childlike and gave the text a lightness which allowed it to balance the vivid colours she used (C36). Between them, the *Tim* and *Orlando* books brought a fresh element into the British nursery that threatened the older concepts of fluffy kittens and prancing elves that had been favoured for so long.

In Australia too, the Picture book established a hold in the 1930s when Dorothy Wall wrote and illustrated the first of the adventures of 'Blinky Bill', the Koala Bear. Her earlier illustrations had been not unlike those of Charles Folkard and other illustrators who had been influenced by Arthur Rackham. They gave little indication of her originality. By 1933, when the *Blinky Bill* books began to appear, her art was more mature and fundamentally serious (133). Despite Blinky Bill's patched trousers, or the expressions of horror on the faces of the various animals she included, Dorothy Wall's art was never frivolous. Her drawings had a conciseness and precision that made them, in a sense, older than the stories to which they belonged. Blinky Bill became a favourite even outside Australia. He has appeared on children's china; in a tea set made by Falcon's, and has even been used as a motif on an engraved silver christening cup. It says much for his popularity that, even after Dorothy Wall's death in 1942, the adventures have been carried on in colour by Walter Stackpool and Stephen Axelsen and that, in this new form, a nursery fabric has been created in his honour.

With the acceptance of the Picture book, no matter whether it depicted the realistic world of Tim or the dionysiac cavortings of Orlando, illustration for the nursery became specific rather than being rolled out as a continuous band of sentimentality, to be snipped off in suitable lengths for yet another Bumper book. Good Picture books have never been common, but where an artist-storyteller could express himself in both words and pictures with equal facility, the results confirm that in the Picture book the art of the nursery book has reached an ideal form.

CHAPTER 13

Nurseries after World War 1

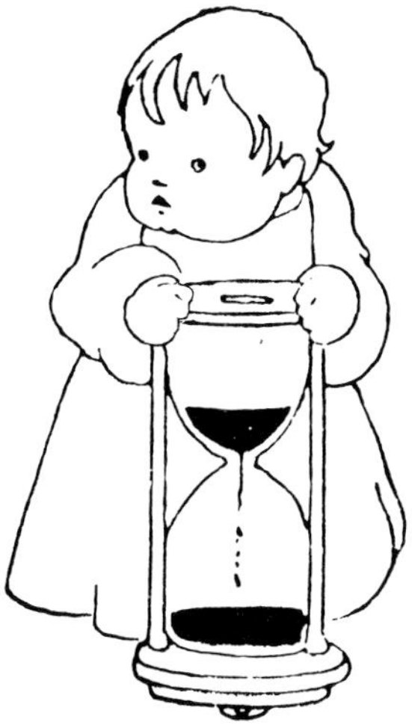

In the years between the turn of the century and World War I the nursery itself was still given scant consideration in house design. This was surprising because, although families, and therefore homes, had become smaller, the concept of the nursery had become more a part of the thinking of even the less affluent.

Where it did exist, the nursery was still largely looked upon as a repository for unwanted items of household furniture. It gave the child his first experience of the 'hand-me-down'. Designers were attempting to urge the public to take the decoration of the nursery seriously. They argued that the world in which the child was to spend such a great proportion of his formative years should reflect his special needs and interests. They felt that it was important that the child should be allowed to escape from the oppressiveness of the dark woodwork and black leading of the cast-iron firegrate that had enveloped a previous generation of children. *The Studio*, that pace-setter of modern thinking in the decorative arts, was strangely equivocal in its approach towards modern nursery design. It gave its approval to a design for a nursery carried out in 1901 by Herbert and Frances MacNair in the clean lines and light colours of the type of furniture that the Glasgow School were then producing (174). By contrast, though, as late as 1914, it criticized a nursery designed in Paris by André Hellé and his wife, very much in the same Glasgow style, for being too advanced for its time (175).

Despite the decorative accretions of Art Nouveau the history of furnishing, as of all the visual arts, from Victorian times to the present day has, with minor interruptions, been one of increasing simplification. The

Hellé nursery showed this in its plain pink walls disturbed only by a Cinderella frieze running round the room at a low eye-level. The room had fitted carpets and full length curtains to guard against the draughts. The drop-sided cot had off-white surfaces to match the woodwork of the room and was decorated with a simple motif that was picked up by the other items of furniture. The whole design was unfussy and helped give the nursery an air of spaciousness and cleanliness that was meant to appeal to the modern hygiene-minded mother.

In complete contrast a nursery designed by Oskar Kaufman in Germany in 1923 with fairy tales as its theme, was a modern reinterpretation of rococo (176). It was a dream nursery for a fairy tale princess and, in its way, a triumph of almost edible fancy. The plaques in relief around the walls depicted scenes from fairy stories, and the tiled continental stove, in pale green, had over it a figure of Hans Andersen's 'Little Chimney Sweep'. The ceiling was equally unusual in that it extended beyond the cornices to form billowing clouds, and from it was suspended a light-fitting with little toy animals hanging from the rim. The very ornate furniture was rose-coloured with inset panels of a brighter pink. It was a

174 Nursery designed by Herbert and Frances MacNair, 1901.

175 (above) Nursery designed by André Hellé, Paris, 1914.

176 (left) Nursery designed by Oscar Kaufman, Berlin, 1923.

C33 (opposite above) Wall picture, *Little Bo-Peep*, 1935.

C34 (opposite below) The Pooh toys, *c.* 1924. Collection of E.P. Dutton Inc., New York.

room that could have been managed only with servant help, but for a child to have grown up in it was Paradise.

This was a unique example. The trend of the post-war years, as had been foreseen by the more advanced designers before the war, was to react against what was looked on by them as the undemanding complacency of public taste. In 1913 Roger Fry, in the showrooms of his Omega Workshops in Fitzroy Square had exhibited his ideas for a nursery (177). He himself had designed the chairs, Duncan Grant the large wooden toys with movable limbs, and Vanessa Bell and Winifred Gill the painted murals of animals and trees done in a style that anticipated by some twenty years the paper cut-outs of Matisse. Even the ceiling was included in the scheme of decoration for, as Vanessa Bell stated, this was the one surface that a baby looked at most when lying flat on its back.

177 Nursery designed by Duncan Grant and Vanessa Bell for the Omega Workshops, 1913.

By the 1920s, whatever was larger than life had to be deflated to match a world that had just undergone a war which, if it was about anything, was about aggrandisement. The war had sharpened both visions and angles. The smooth curves of Art Nouveau were replaced by the jaggedness of Art Deco, softness was replaced by brashness, languor by alertness and heavenly lengths by terseness.

Art Deco, that inelegant child of Cubism and Art Nouveau, reached its apogee in the 1930s and proved to be hardly more suited to design for the nursery than Art Nouveau had been. The cumbersome solidity of the style was at odds with the grace and lightness of the furniture that had tried to change the image of the nursery just after World War I. The

LAWSON WOOD.

designer Gabriel Englinger, in Paris in 1931, attempted to be both fashionable and simple, but the Deco style imposed such a bulkiness on his furniture that its mobility was lost in the striving for overall effect (178).

C35 Lawson Wood: 'Old Mother Hubbard' from *The Lawson Wood Nursery Rhyme Book*, Thomas Nelson & Sons Ltd., 1933.

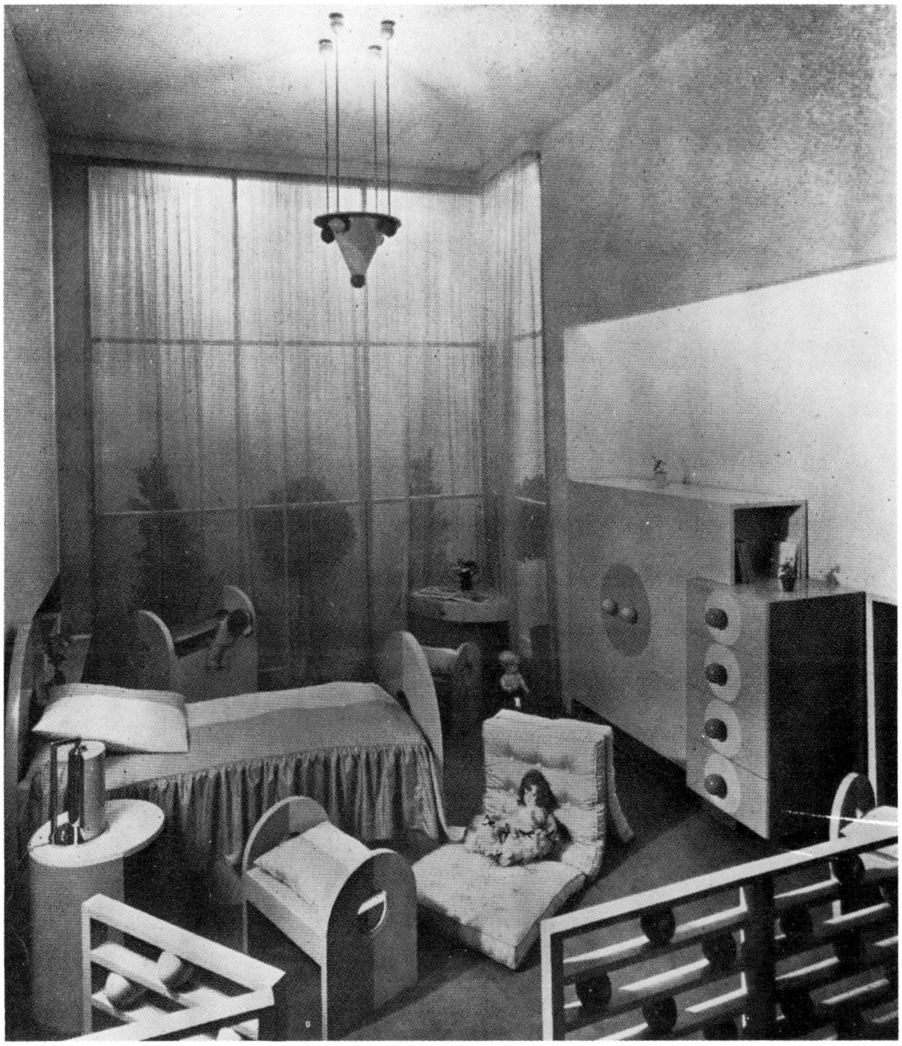

178 Nursery designed by Gabriel Englinger, Paris, 1932.

Similarly, the most modern and impressive feature of Robert Heller's nursery of 1937 – a white cot trimmed in fire-engine red – was, unfortunately, the one incongruous feature in an otherwise successful room (179).

The 'thirties were also the years of exploration of the use of new materials, when tubular metal, as well as the early plastics, were being tried out. If the skeletal furniture designed by the Czech, K. Orta, appears nowadays to have a stark clinical air, one must accept that the medium was a new one, and that its very novelty was its attraction (180).

Patterned fabrics, rather than wallpaper, were used to bring colour into the nurseries, and printed curtains and bed covers became important features of nursery decor (181). Designs were both abstract and pictorial.

179 (right) Night nursery, designed by Robert Heller, 1937.

180 (below) Nursery, designed by K.E. Orta, Prague, 1931.

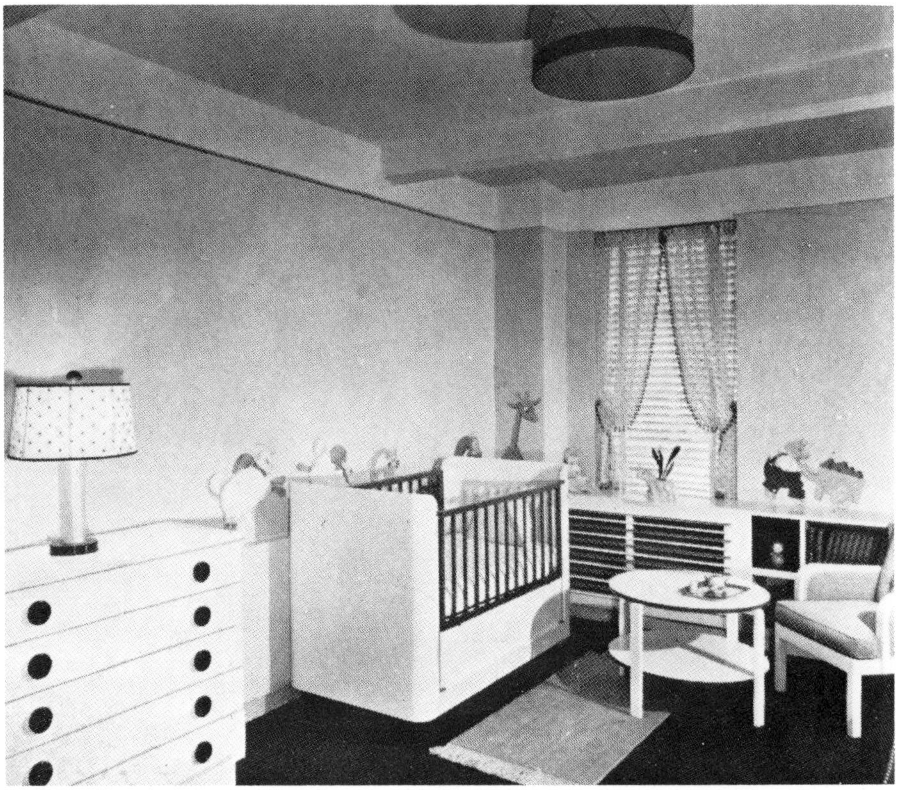

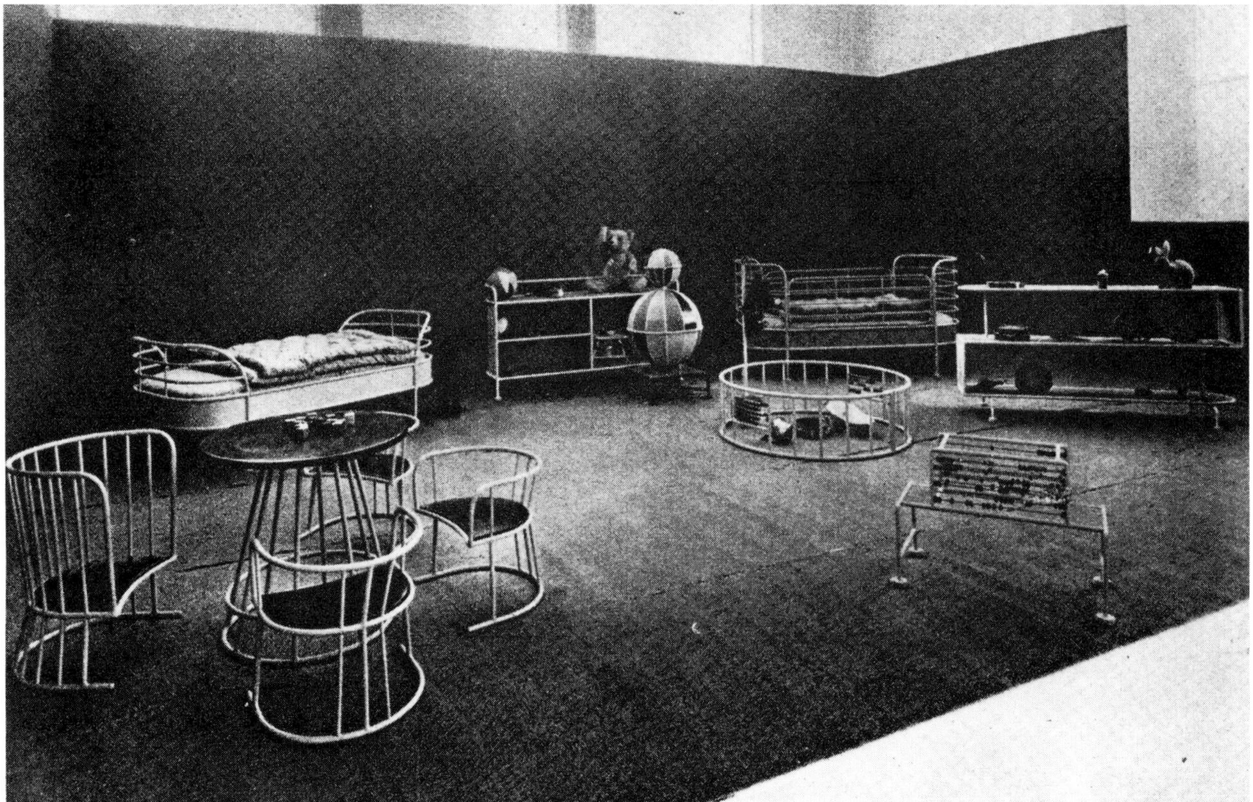

Some had scattered motifs set against plain coloured backgrounds, while others had more organized patterns. These were the days of Charles Voysey's 'Alice' fabric; May Gibbs's 'Gumnuts'; and Otto Messmer's 'Felix the Cat' - a rebellious product of the 'twenties and 'thirties who in addition to being featured in comic strips, books and on nursery china, was also the hero of a number of animated films (182).

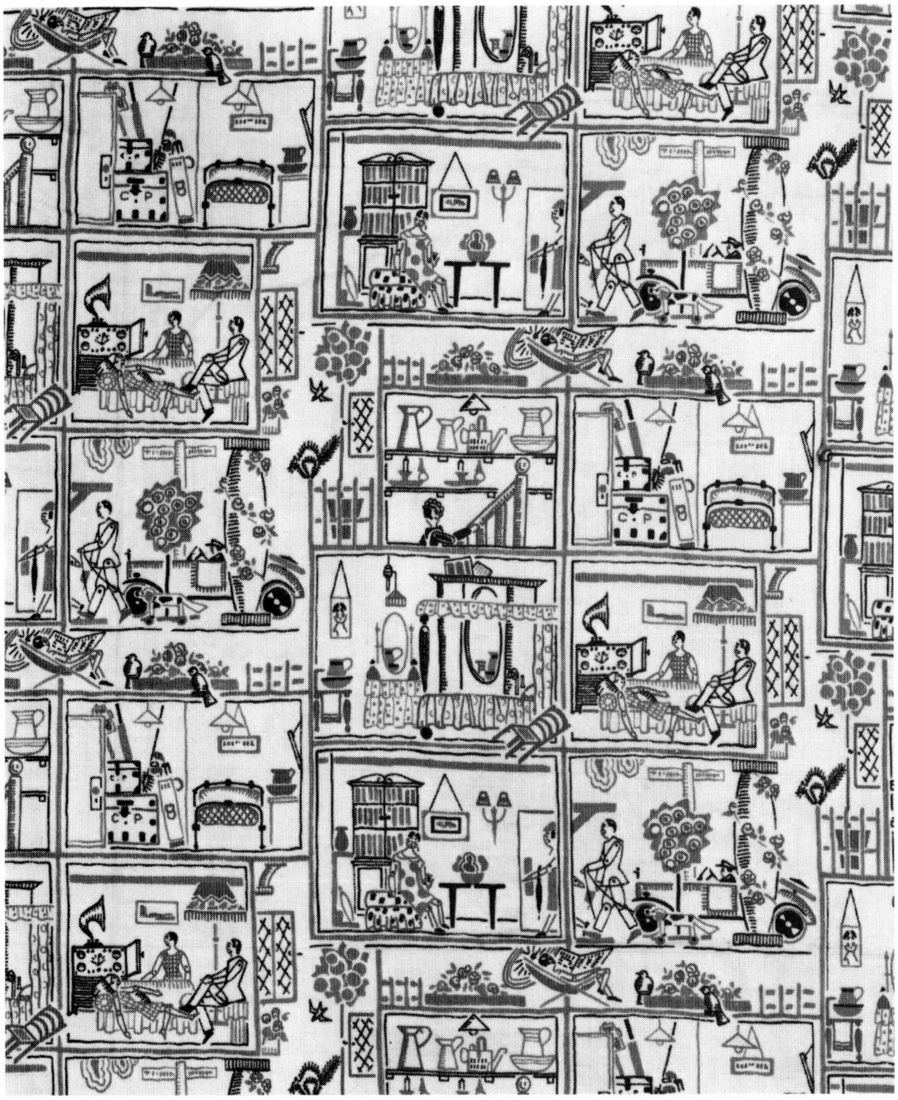

181 (left) Nursery fabric: 'The Doll's House', printed cotton by Tootal, 1930. Victoria & Albert Museum.

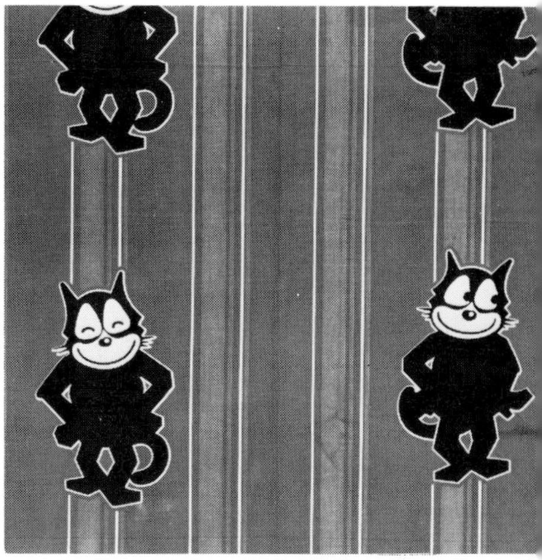

182 (above) Nursery fabric: 'Felix the Cat', designed by Otto Messmer, 1924. Victoria & Albert Museum.

More thought was also given to the improvement of those fabric designs which incorporated the standard nursery themes of soldiers, toys, circuses or the nursery rhyme characters. A particularly notable series was designed for Marionette Prints by the Guatemala-born artist Tony Sarg, who had a long and successful career as an illustrator, especially of nursery Trick books, in both Britain and the United States (C37). In general, fabric design for the nursery in the 'thirties was more successful than

183 Nursery, designed by Pierre Dutel, New York, 1937.

wallpaper design because the fabrics always used stylization, and avoided the poor attempts at naturalistic reproduction that so often spoilt wallpapers before the introduction of modern photolithography.

Nursery wallpaper design was hardly affected by the Art Deco movement, apart from the almost mandatory use of jazzy Aztec patterned borders. Shortly before World War II wallpaper went out of fashion and, for a number of years, walls were merely painted or decorated with plaster scumble. Coloured transfers were used to enliven the plain surfaces, with enthusiasm occasionally overreaching itself, as in the nursery designed in New York in 1937 by Pierre Dutel (183). Here, the striped ceiling with the mirror glass light fitting, the bold multicoloured floor covering and the mural of *trompe l'oeil* alphabet blocks hurtling out of the wall, seemed turbulent and disturbing in its restlessness.

The trend away from the use of wallpaper was reinforced by the wartime shortage of woodpulp. In 1945, concerned that even with the restoration of supplies after the war there might still be insufficient interest in the use of wallpaper, the Central Institute of Art and Design promoted an exhibition of the best pre-war papers, together with a number of newly commissioned designs. Graham Sutherland, Edmund Dulac, Mabel Lucie Attwell and other well-known artists were invited to contribute. Dulac, in 1923, had decorated the walls of the night nursery in the Queen's Dolls' House with fairy tales done in the familiar style of his book illustrations. His new wallpaper, of scenes from nursery rhymes, was a curious and somewhat atypical work (184). He dressed the characters in contemporary clothes, making Jack Horner, Little Tommy Stout and Jack and Jill look quite incongruous in a shirt or blouse, shorts, school shoes and socks. The use of flat stylized flowers to separate the vignettes added to the stiffness of the design. Typically, Dulac carried out research into the whole mechanism of wallpaper printing, and made detailed notes at the bottom of the design in his beautiful handwriting. The wallpaper, though, had a detached air and lacked spontaneity. What was missing was a sense of joy, and this was equally true of a superb toy elephant he designed. His templates were measured, drawn and cut out with the greatest care, but the pursuit of perfection that bedevilled him throughout his life denied him the air of whimsy that was required. The result was a sensitively observed, but decidedly uncuddly toy.

In the years leading up to, and immediately following World War II, the quality of wallpaper design varied considerably. Some papers, in attempting to renew traditional designs were surprisingly crude. In others, well-known story book characters suffered in translation from the original idiom to wallpaper. Rupert Bear was particularly unfortunate in this respect. Only later, when new photolithographic printing techniques were introduced, were Bugs Bunny, Walt Disney's Pooh, Paddington Bear and the Mister Men able to make the transition successfully.

184 Edmund Dulac: design for nursery wallpaper, pencil and watercolour, 1945. Private collection.

The most effective wallpapers have always been those in which the pictorial elements have been treated as symbols, and arranged in patterns of decoration rather than set as narrative. One paper, 'Oranges and Lemons' designed in this way by Dorothy Hilton as long ago as 1902, still looks decidedly modern (12), (185). Designs like this succeed or fail purely on the appeal of the arrangement of their motifs, and the standard of decoration of these papers in Britain in the post-war years, whether the designs have been built up of stylized animals, people or merely abstract forms, has been consistently high (186). The papers, and a more recently introduced accessory of matching fabrics, have been both original and exhilarating. A modern Sanderson's paper, 'The Teddy Bears' Picnic' is a fine example of an overall pattern that has retained its cheerfulness and modernity while, at the same time, avoiding the claustrophobic oppressiveness of the French wallpaper of toys of a century earlier (C38).

American nursery wallpapers have, on the whole, been disappointing.

One factor has been the fall in demand, because the walls of so many children's rooms have become plain surfaces for the display of posters, pictures, banners and photographs. The nursery papers manufactured there have often been gaudy and insensitive. Coarse reproductions of pages from comics, and assemblages of cars, ships, aeroplanes and guns, often tastelessly embellished with a coloured metallic reflecting finish, have overshadowed those few papers, such as Margaret Owen's 'In the Country', in which good design has been allowed expression (187).

The one motif that has remained unfailingly popular in wallpaper design, whether pre- or post-war, has been Mickey Mouse. No single character created by anybody in any idiom has achieved such world-wide recognition. From the time of his creation by Walt Disney in 1928, when he was a cruder and very different Mickey from the one we know, he has endeared himself to children of all ages and all nations. Mickey is unique: his ears are always drawn as if seen from the front no matter which way he is actually facing; his shoes are like cushions, into which no legs, however spindly, could ever have fitted; and his gloves, like his shoes, were necessary to solve the problem of what to do with his paws. The gloves provided him with hands and fingers to use like a human's, but more subtle and far-reaching than this was the fact that the gloves determined Mickey's status. No rapscallion would ever wear gloves like these. Mickey, by this one stroke, was given authority. He was the one who, even though he might not be listened to at first, would prove to be right. Mickey and his wife Minnie were the epitome of anthropomorphism. They were likeable, instantly recognizable and, because of the international language of moving pictures, were accepted unreservedly throughout the world.

The Disney organization was not slow to realize the potential of their creation, and Mickey Mouse invaded the nursery in many diverse forms (188). The first Annual appeared in 1931, and the images of Mickey and his friends Donald Duck, Pluto, Goofy and so many others, decorated toys, toothbrushes, nightlights, money boxes, soap, china, napkins, transfers for the wall and for the backs of small hands, watches and sweets. Mickey's image is both universal and eternal. He is the standard against which other examples of the cartoonist's art on film is judged.

All cartoon art is based on the distillation of the essence of an image. The animated cartoon intensifies the presentation and the presence of that form and, in so doing, has become the main propagandist for the Hollywood weakness for 'cuteness'. The genius of Walt Disney was that he realized the power of this type of stylization to concentrate an image and make its impact irresistible. In 1937 he presented Snow White as the complete princess. She was the American ideal of the 'girl next door' and a fitting model for every American child to aspire to because she was every parent's unfulfilled dream. Similarly, Disney's square-jawed, thick-necked prince in *The Sleeping Beauty* was the symbol of the total hero: a

185 (opposite) Nursery wallpaper: 'Oranges and Lemons' by Dorothy Hilton, 1902. Bradford Art Galleries and Museums.

186 Nursery wallpaper: 'Zoo', Crown Decorative Products Ltd., 1975.

187 Nursery wallpaper: 'In the Country', Margowen Inc., New York, 1979.

pattern for every nursery child to grow into or to marry. And Dopey, whose inability to cope with the problems of the everyday world endeared him to even the youngest child, was the essence of the lovable schlemiel. Each character was a symbol. Each symbol had a set of attributes that amounted to a personality. But each personality was a depersonalization because, in aiming for the simplest generalization and the widest appeal, there was filtered out anything that might have drawn attention away from the qualities being advertised. The characters were too true to type for their types to be real.

The very simplification of the message that the animated cartoon pro-

vided meant that there was greater ease of understanding for the child. When little tokens of this magic entered the nursery, from rattles to bed covers, the child was given to understand that he was surrounded by ready-made friends. The victory of the animated-cartoon characters in the nursery was one of natural selection. There developed an industry that by its world-wide distribution and universality of its images, drove out of the nursery all but the most resilient characters of the pre-animated cartoon days. Pooh, Teddy and Golly survived, to be joined now by Goofy, Horace Horsecollar, Donald, Pluto and, of course, Mickey and Minnie. The others atrophied by disuse.

Other film companies and animators tried to match Disney's success. Max Fleischer invented 'Betty Boop' – a walking, talking cutie-doll and, even more successfully, the endearing character of 'Popeye'. Warner Brothers produced their 'Bugs Bunny' and 'Tom and Jerry' cartoons, but the sheer enormity of the Disney organization and the quality of its products ensured that it remained the standard for all to be judged by. Barriers of race and language were overcome and, at the time, it looked as if the movie cartoon characters had taken over the nursery. The reign seemed firm and unshakeable. In fact its supremacy lasted for barely a decade before its position was challenged by the more intimate and persuasive claims of television. Even then the makers of animated cartoons attempted to maintain their dominion over children's taste by distributing their wares in bulk to television companies.

The accusation against the American animated cartoons of tastelessness and indulgence in sentimentality merely acknowledged the fact that the ultimate simplicity of image and message had been achieved. If slickness was often in evidence at the expense of charm, its influence and possibly its value in the nursery has been greater because slickness could be parcelled into units whereas the less concrete concepts of charm or poetic fancy could not. The child is not able to grasp the significance of the evanescent, whereas the realistic can be, and has been, made attractive by being dressed in magic clothes. Subtlety is for those with a library of experience to refer to. Fantasy does not always have to be synonymous with the ephemeral. The animated cartoon succeeded in the nursery because its images were fresh, its colours lively and its messages easy to understand. Because of this, Mickey Mouse wallpaper and Donald Duck transfers became the surroundings that most children woke up to in the nurseries of the late 'thirties and 'forties to wash their faces with Pluto soap and brush their teeth with a Goofy toothbrush. Only the crabbed of heart could claim that the force was for anything but good.

188 Nursery tea plate: 'Mickey and Minnie', © Walt Disney Enterprises; diameter 6 in. Private collection.

CHAPTER 14

The 'Contemporary' Nursery

The 1939–1945 war solved, for its duration, the problem of unemployment. For the first time, people who would have aimed no higher in their lives than a position in domestic service were given a sense of dignity and self-importance. They were now serving a cause greater than that of a single family. Before the war a housemaid was an accepted feature of a middle-class home. After the war, living-in servants were rarely to be found. Night and Day nurseries could not survive without them. Even the nursery suite had to be eliminated as a result of government restrictions on the permitted size of new buildings, and of the shortage of materials. The term 'nursery' became, first, the name for a child's bedroom, and then came to refer to the communal crèche where working mothers deposited their children during the day. Paradoxically, this change of emphasis succeeded, not so much in downgrading the nursery, as in making it more personal. 'John's Room' or 'Jane's Room' seemed to offer a more embracing warmth than 'The Nursery', which never quite lost the feeling of alienation that years of exposure to more rigid forms of upbringing had given it. 'Nursery' implied a distancing and a sense of 'there'. 'Jane's Room' offered a sense of enfolding and a feeling of 'here'.

If the drabness of the immediate post-war years in Britain was the outward sign of a weakened country struggling to its feet, the return to normality was helped by one of the most enlightened acts ever carried out by a British Government.

The Festival of Britain, intended originally as an acknowledgment of the centenary of the first of the World Fairs, the Great Exhibition of 1851, enlivened the country with its brilliance. No exhibition since 'Paris 1900', that showcase for Art Nouveau, had such an influence on the taste of a generation. By example, it instilled, especially in the young, an enthusiasm for new design that seemed, after twelve years of austerity, to have been conceived in a world of the future. It was, in fact, an exhibition on a popular level of all that had been in the avant garde of design in the years immediately preceding the war. It heralded the age of 'Contemporary' and was attuned to the optimism of the newly demobilized servicemen who were setting up home for the first time. It was a visible manifestation of a national sigh of relief.

In marking the end of rationing, the Exhibition turned its back on 'Utility' and the strict functionalism of wartime products, and indulged in the delights of decoration as an adjunct to design. Fabrics, furniture,

189 Esmé Eve: 'Jack and Jill' from *Mother Goose Nursery Rhymes*, Blackie & Sons Ltd., 1955.

china and the illustrations in nursery books all expressed a gaiety, in both colour and form, that had been absent for so long (189).

JACK AND JILL WENT UP THE HILL
To fetch a pail of water.
Jack fell down and broke his crown,
And Jill came tumbling after.
Then up Jack got and home did trot,
As fast as he could caper;
Went to bed to mend his head,
With vinegar and brown paper.
VINEG

The new 'Contemporary' was a leggy fashion (190). Nursery furniture stood on rods bent into 'V' or 'W' shapes, or balanced unsteadily on slender cones of new silky anodysed metal. Little coloured balls like cocktail cherries were much in evidence as knobs or stands. Furniture design recaptured its simplicity, and 'space' and 'circulation' were correct words to use (191). Novel shapes like the 'Coolie' chair (192) and materials used in unexpected ways, as in the rocking-horse of cane (193), attempted to be original within this basic principle. Lightness became synonymous with brightness, and was emphasized by the introduction of versatile laminated plastics which brought to the nursery a strong, attractive,

child-resistant material that could be used for any surface. Gaily coloured rugs and curtains in interesting patterns gave warmth and variety of texture to rooms that might otherwise have been clinical looking.

The Festival of Britain celebrated the arrival of the Atomic Age, and the pattern on fabrics, plastics and paper related to the new belief in Science as the panacea for the sickness of mankind. Stylized abstractions of natural forms which appeared on nursery curtains and wallpapers, had their origins in crystals and seeds, seashells and string diagrams. Designs were inspired by the world seen under the microscope, by the moons of Joan Miro and by those lines that Paul Klee used to take out for walks. They had a versatility that allowed them to serve equally well in the nursery or the kitchen, and few exclusively children's motifs were used. If occasionally the colours sang too loudly and the decor accosted the child rather than soothed him, it was at least a time when people were encouraged to take notice of their surroundings. The concept of good design and fitness for purpose was stressed everywhere, and became accepted with fervour as if it were a newly discovered truth.

Although the spindly designs, delicately coloured, patterned with lozenges and scalloped at the edges, proved to be no more than a temporary fashion – mere appendages to the spirit of being 'modern' – the 'Contemporary' period brought to the nursery one new kind of decoration, simple,

190 (above) Bassinet, cane on metal stand, lined in pale blue and yellow nylon, height 27 in., manufactured by Heal & Son Ltd., 1961.

191 (right) Bed, designed by Frank Guille, DesRCA, FSIAD, as a christening present for Prince Charles from the Royal College of Art, 1950. The silver inlaid enamelled escutcheons designed by Philip Popham. The bed was made of steam-bent yew by Ron Lenthall.

192 (left) Child's chair, inverted 'coolie hat', bamboo on metal frame, Heal & Son Ltd., 1961.

193 (below) Nursery furniture, Heal & Son Ltd., 1950–2.

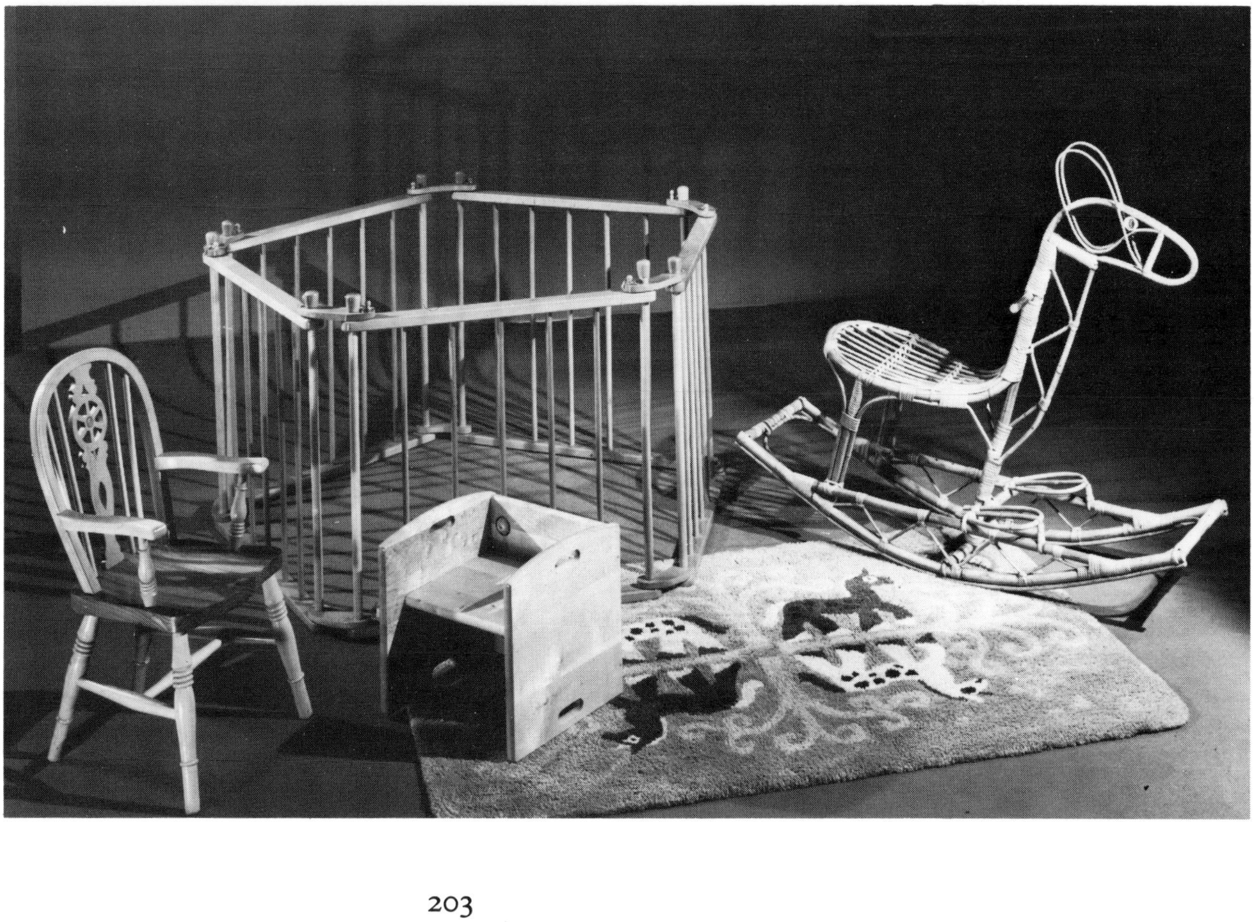

194 Nursery, designed by Iimar Tapiovaara, Finland, 1960.

cheap and totally original. Alexander Calder could hardly have realized how much a household name his sculptures, the 'Mobiles', would become, and how many ingenious variations on his original plates of painted steel could be made. Birds of wood and boats of feathers; angels of straw; discs of coloured plastic or glass; plain and fanciful decorations of all kinds, provided a fascinating amalgam of toy and art-form for all ages.

The Studio magazine and the firm of Liberty had been synonymous with Art Nouveau in Great Britain. 'Contemporary' had its equivalent in the magazine *House and Garden* and Heal's, where their espousal of the new styles in both British and Continental design had an unrivalled influence on the appearance of children's rooms. In the United States, on the other hand, wartime shortages had been less acute, and there had been no equivalent force imposed from the outside to compel a change in traditional tastes. Both the manufacturers and the public were more fixed in their ways and did not immediately accept the new styles so that, for a number of years, most of the 'Contemporary' designs in America were imported from Europe.

By the early 'sixties some designers were moving away from what they felt was merely a restatement of the more enlightened ideas of the pre-war years, and adopted an even greater simplicity of form (194). In Britain the style became that of Conran and the house of Habitat, with nursery furniture unadorned, but beautifully finished, in lightly varnished natural woods. Nursery accessories of mugs and bowls were manufactured in a contrasting style that recreated Victorian or Edwardian extravagances of lettering, motif and design. Both approaches were attempts to escape from what was now felt to be the tyranny of a technology that had leaped beyond the comprehension of the layman. It represented a growing fear of science and the ever present threat of nuclear war. It was a desire to turn back from a world that had become too impersonal to what was felt to have been the greater humaneness of the years at the beginning of the century. The change coincided with a growing interest in natural foods and the manufacture of utensils having an almost folk-like simplicity. Enamelled jugs and beakers had 'Baby' written on their sides in large,

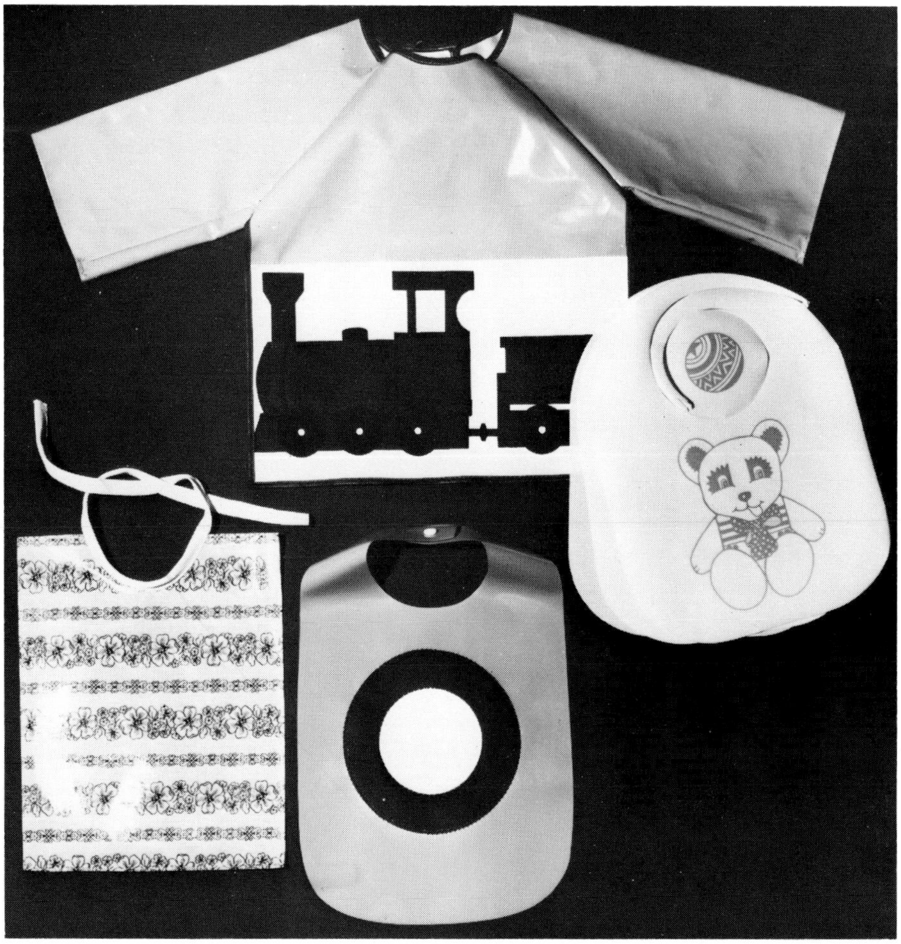

195 Shifts, feeders and aprons, Heal & Son Ltd., 1968.

old-fashioned letters. The plastic Donald Duck potty reverted to the traditional white enamelled basin-shape with a thin blue line round the rim. It became sophisticated to appear unsophisticated. A gesture had been made, but the enlarged reproduction on a baby's mug of an old wood engraving of 'Three Blind Mice' could provide only a temporary escape from an insuperable problem. More violently true to its time was the all-plastic bath of 1972, in which the total refinement of the object from all non-essentials left a 'Brave New World' effect which, when compared with the lush prodigality of the bath of 1851 seemed a very meagre offering for the nursery (195), (196), (13). 'Sterility' has more than one meaning and, sadly, in attempting the one, it was not always possible to escape the other. The answer lay somewhere between the two extremes. Perhaps the desire to 'grace' the nursery was the missing factor.

196 Cradle-bath, perspex, Heal & Son Ltd., 1972.

CHAPTER 15

Television and the Nursery

Before the war television had been in its infancy and was a luxury for the few. Its potential had scarcely been realized. After the war it became an absolute requirement of every home and a uniting feature of family life. However much it enforced a rethinking of one's way of looking at that unity, it developed into a nucleus around which the home revolved. It became both an educative medium and a source of propaganda directed towards the child. It affected the design and decoration of the nursery, and played a large part in destroying its already enfeebled existence. Outside those last bastions of resident nannies, where television, although a comfort and a solace, was often a convenient way of excluding an employee, however much loved, from the bosom of the family, the effect was one of further undermining the separateness of the child's world from that of the parents. Because the family television was kept in the living-room the child came back into this common-room, and what the nursery lost in individuality the family gained in unity.

In television the parents found a teacher, a nanny and a tempter eager to fill the child with ready-packed delights. As was true of the animated cartoons, the way characters looked was no longer determined by the child's imagination. Their forms were dictated rather than suggested. Consequently, television restricted the depth of taste and thought as much as it expanded the range.

Books and films retreated before this advance. Some achieved assimilation by being shown as adaptations, but many nursery favourites disappeared in confusion in the face of television's seductive and irresistible invasion. Parents expressed concern and educationalists raged. The unacceptable images provided by certain types of books and films that had once aroused their wrath were forgiven and forgotten in the face of the new enemy. The noble ethic stated that whatever had to be sought after was more worthwhile than what was being presented piecemeal. Gratification was directly related to effort. Suddenly, the battle cries of parents against the reading of comics and similar 'rubbish' were silenced in the face of the even more harmful horrors of mindless exposure to the ever-present television programmes. Television was looked upon as a Pandora's box ready to disgorge, at the press of a button, its nefarious contents into the susceptible minds of defenceless children. Sociologists cringed before the black magic of its immediate delights. All of which was to overlook any sense of responsibility on the part of the programme planners.

In the United States, where television was already established, there was no national network that was independent of commercial considerations. Size of audience, and hence of sales, was of major importance to a sponsor. The result was an almost pandemic use of the very same animated cartoon shorts that had been the mainstay of news cinemas for several years. By contrast, in Great Britain, both the British Broadcasting Corporation and the Independent Television Authority showed a sense of responsibility towards the contents of children's programmes that set an example to the rest of the world; so much so, in fact, that the very supremacy of the children's comic, let alone the printed page as a means of communication with children, had ultimately to be called into question. Although any undermining effect of television on total literacy has not been very significant, a change in the age at which reading for pleasure commences will probably be noticed in time. There are, however, compensations. The inventiveness of television programmes has been of a high order. Very many new characters have been created for a child's delight and, as if by some universal levelling process, a number of these have been given an extra dimension in book form.

As with any other medium involving the nursery, an essential ingredient for the success of a television series has always been the creation of a unique character with an individual personality. 'Muffin the Mule' and 'The Woodentops' of the 1950s, 'Sooty' the teddy bear conjurer, and the widely popular 'Bill and Ben' the flowerpot men, all of whom had books of their adventures published, are strong childhood memories for people now with children of their own. Each new series introduced fresh characters whose universal appeal then became evident in the nursery in the form of toys, shaped soaps, bubble baths, toothbrushes and, significantly, books (C39). The characters had attributes and images that had been refined to the essentials. They were independent of time or place, and this allowed the best of them to be re-introduced to another generation of children without loss of impact.

Charm seems to be important for the success of any new television character. This is something that is understood by the very young even if they cannot put a name to the quality. It is as if the concept of charm were bound up with the intimacy of watching television with mother. *The Magic Roundabout* has charm in abundance, and its status as a cult following in the student world is evidence of its persuasiveness. Its characters have appeared in books in both French and English, and posters of them for nursery walls and transfers for nursery furniture have had remarkable sales. Its success as a programme has been due to its unfailing honesty to the child and to its imaginative, cheerfully coloured sets. Even when translated into book form, with the pages often divided into slabs of print and picture, the artwork of Serge Danot is so delightful that 'What happens next?' belongs almost as much to the pictures as to the story (197). The basis of its charm is its total lack of aggression, something that is equally true of the series featuring the clown doll 'Andy Pandy'. His adventures, too, have appeared in books, both of the annual type, with illustrations by Phil Gascoine, and in the true Picture book type with pictures by Matvyn Wright. Gascoine's illustrations are brash and extrovert, and make the books ideal for occasional and exciting dipping. Matvyn Wright's are more poised and are ideal for quiet nursery reading (198). Each serves its purpose admirably.

Television has been of the nature of a vast stock exchange. It provides products for translation into other media and can itself transform material

197 Serge Danot: 'Florence and Dougal', from *The Magic Roundabout*, Dean and Son Ltd., 1972.

198 Matvyn Wright: illustration from *Andy Pandy's Weather House* by Maria Bird, Hodder & Stoughton.

that had first appeared in other forms into television images. 'Worzel Gummidge', the lovable scarecrow with the interchangeable heads, a 'Thinking Head' and a 'Scaring Head', who had long been a favourite on the radio programme *Children's Hour* and in subsequent books of his adventures, took colourful and solid shape on television. Enid Blyton's 'Noddy', a latter-day Pinocchio, who has been illustrated by several artists in books and children's comics, has become a popular television character, as have Rupert Bear and his friends. The even more imaginative Paddington Bear, the hero of Michael Bond's books, in addition to becoming a television favourite, has decorated china and a nursery alarm clock, been used as a wallpaper design, as writing paper and, even more impressively, been used like Outcault's 'Tige', as a trade symbol in shops selling a certain brand of children's rainwear (56).

Children's programmes on American television have been of a different order. Many have relied on ready-made animated cartoon films which, while slick and attractive, and often very funny, are all too often based on the principle of outsmarting an adversary. The animal puppets of Captain Kangaroo are an isolated and noteworthy exception to the almost total replacement of charm and sensibility by cuteness and cunning. Perhaps Kermit and the woolly monsters of the Muppets and Sesame Street are the compromises that have to be accepted in this competitive field (199). While 'Bugs Bunny' and 'Tom and Jerry' have always been favourites on both the cinema and television screens, it has been the indigenous television characters who have won the affection of the nursery child. Sharing the continuity of a series with a parent, and with the adventures directed

199 Tom Cooke: 'One day Ernie was coming home . . .' from *Cookie Monster's Story Book*, Random House Inc., 1979. © 1983 Children's Television Workshop. Used by permission of Children's Television Workshop.

C36 (opposite) Kathleen Hale: 'Orlando gave a Party', from *Orlando the Marmalade Cat – A Trip Abroad*, Country Life, London, 1949. © Kathleen Hale.

C37 (overleaf, left) Nursery fabric. Tony Sarg: 'Wooden Toys', printed cotton, manufactured by Marionette Prints, 1936. Cooper-Hewitt Museum, New York.

C38 (overleaf, right) Nursery wallpaper, 'The Teddy Bears' Picnic', Sanderson & Co., 1978.

towards his particular age group rather than attempting to entertain at all levels, as the cartoons do, the child is given a special relationship with his favourite characters. Small people hearken best to small voices, and it is the intimate and persuasive that makes a greater appeal than the hectoring.

And then, suddenly, as if to confound the prophets of doom, it was realized that, concurrently with the rise of television, there had dawned a new Golden Age of children's book illustration. The expanding fields of television and advertising had need for a large number of graphic artists and designers. Many brought with them experience of work on animated films. All were aware of the latest advances in graphic art, innovations quickly became common property and techniques and ideas were exchanged internationally. The involvement of many of these artists in book illustration was a natural outcome of their work, and an attractive style developed that could be reproduced by offset-lithography with greater truth to the original artwork and with greater ease than had been possible in the past.

Sometimes one word sounds
the same as another
like hair and hare
or pair and pear.

200 Paul Rand: 'Sometimes one word sounds the same as another', from *Sparkle and Spin* by Ann and Paul Rand, Harcourt Brace, and Collins, 1957.

The standard was extremely high but, at first, illustrations looked interchangeable. The angular stylized figures with El Greco faces often had a sameness about them, as if one prolific illustrator were working under different names in many different countries. There were recognizable similarities between contemporary illustrations in Britain, Europe and America. All the illustrations were very beautiful, the technique was admirable, the imagination was breathtaking and the colours were delightful, but in a world touched by Midas one longed for a single green leaf.

Individuality gradually asserted itself. The wonderful Dr Seuss books, still owing much to the imagery of animated cartoons, made learning to read a hilarious adventure with their wild and exciting illustrations that

Orlando Gives A Party.
(Chapter 5)

Yogi
bubble bath
THE SPONGE MR
MR BOUNCE
HOLLY HOBBIE
I'M A MR FORGETFUL SPONGE!
DON'T LOSE ME!
Grossmith
The MUPPET SHOW
Bubble Bath
170 ml
bubbly bath
52cc

f
a
g

still managed to retain the self-effacement of true Picture books. Some, such as the justly famous *Sparkle and Spin*, which Ann and Paul Rand wrote and illustrated in 1957, moved towards pure abstraction, using shapes and colours with all the wizardry of graphic design (200). This was a type of fantasy that no longer needed a fairy tale as an excuse for an artist to give form to his imagination.

The post-war novel turned to realism. Children's books, on the other hand, having already discovered the limitations of reality, returned to imaginative fantasy. By the early 1960s many new illustrators had come to maturity in Europe, Asia and America, each bringing a quality and variety of work that became something to marvel at. In the United States, the versatility of Maurice Sendak showed itself in work ranging from surrealist creations that had the atmospheric intensity of drawings by Max Ernst, to line drawings that showed a touching naïveté in their simplicity; and, of course *The Night Kitchen* and *Where the Wild Things Are* became classics of children's literature. The coolly exquisite illustrations of Nancy Ekholm Burket stand in total contrast to the explosion of mad cartoon characters that filled Richard Scarry's 'mystery stories for kids'. The traditional world of elves and fairies was newly opened up by Michael Hague, while the love of nature and the simple life was conveyed with warmth and sincerity in the beautiful work of Tasha Tudor.

In Great Britain especially, the new Golden Age took many forms. Unique in output and ability, Edward Ardizzone was the one illustrator whose work survived the war. He had no imitators and the younger illustrators found inspiration in work other than his. Charles Keeping, the foremost of these, shared Ardizzone's superb draughtsmanship, even though he worked in a totally different style. Whether drawing with pen and ink on paper, or illustrating in coloured inks on plastic film in a manner designed to record the fleeting glimpse of things seen in the glare of sunlight through half-closed eyes, his illustrations have a technical expertise and breadth of vision that are unique in contemporary nursery art. In the greatest contrast to this are the Stanley Spencer-like naïvetés of Helen Oxenbury's illustrations, united and compact in the true tradition of the Picture books. Even realism has extended to neo-surrealism in the illusionist pictures of fantasy that Nicola Bayley and William Aldredge have brought to their books. There are many of these new illustrators. What they have in common is the fact that they care about the presentation of their books. Illustrators are no longer content to offer the anonymous art of the 'Mummy's Little Helper' type. A sense of responsibility towards the nursery is evident in their work: one that demands creative pride in bringing to the child a considered joy, free from the self-imposed didacticism of the American Picture books but, at the same time, eschewing a return to the irresponsibility and anarchy that was so evident in the world of children's books between the world wars.

C39 (opposite above) A selection of pharmaceutical products for nursery use.

C40 (opposite below) A Snoopy nursery. © Charles Schulz, 1958, United Feature Syndicate Inc.

The most influential character in the nursery today has come neither from television, films or books but, surprisingly, from the comic strip. The Age of the Child is the Age of Snoopy. Without doubt Snoopy is the first character since Mickey Mouse to have won the hearts of all people everywhere. Philosopher to the grown-up and friend to the child, he, Woodstock and the human pets they have adopted are universally loved. He has invaded the nursery in every form, from fabrics and candles to pictures and mugs. His image and his message of companionableness transcend the boundaries of language, geography and time. His fallibility, his sincerity and his capacity for love, however reconditely expressed, find an echo in all hearts. The Charles Schulz characters have both style and charm. Snoopy could well become immortal, as Mickey Mouse has done. The potential of his image as a force for good, whether for road safety or as an inducement towards tooth brushing, is only just beginning to be recognized. As the nursery dies in its traditional form and becomes just another room in the house, perhaps it will be Snoopy who will provide the continuity between the nursery world and that of the adult. It may be that, in his own way, Snoopy will complete the cycle by bringing the adult back to the magical and often enviable world of the nursery (C40), (201).

201 Charles Schulz: 'Snoopy', © 1958 United Feature Syndicate Inc.

Conclusion

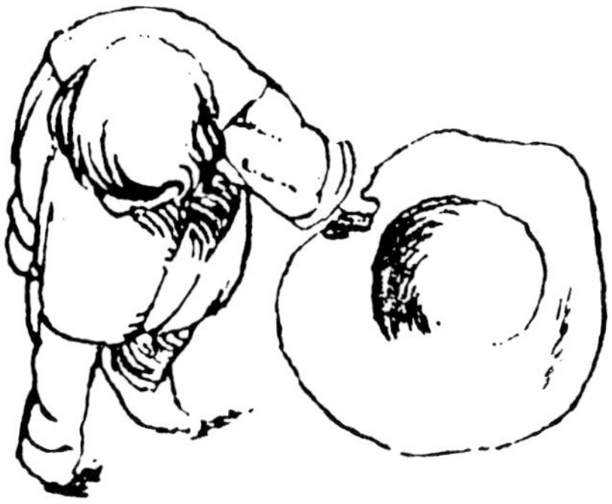

The nursery of Victorian times has gone for ever. The night and day nurseries have contracted to a single room: the abundance of servants to the occasional domestic help and the washing machine. It has decreased in size and increased in simplicity. The very name has become pretentious or, at best, a synonym for 'Play School'. The nursery which, less than a hundred years ago reflected the adult world in its rejected and out-of-date fashions brought up from downstairs has become a room which expresses the world of the child - or, at least, what parents believe the world of the child to be.

The fundamental purpose of art for the nursery has been to give the child a sense of identity and to have him understand that something has been created for his pleasure. Nursery art, whether in the form of decorated alphabets, Noah's Ark friezes or illustrated nursery rhymes, has been used as a palliative for instruction. It has provided the child with images to make friends with, to share his secrets, his loves and his hatreds. It has provided him with reassurances in the form of pictures on the wall whose presence has helped to comfort him when he was sad, or guard him against the evil things of the night. It has been used against him in one-sided games when being washed was less unpleasant if the soap was in the shape of Yogi Bear, or when he has been beguiled into eating otherwise unacceptable food by searching for the bunny at the bottom of his plate. It has been brought into the nursery to add continuity - the desire for permanence of otherwise evanescent delights - so that some of the wonder of a cinema or television character may become assumed by the possession of its image in a tangible form. My Snoopy drinking mug means that he is

MY friend. It has been used to stimulate wonder about the world outside the nursery: an advertising poster for growing up. It has been used as a vanity by the parent in order to express wealth or social aspiration. At its best, nursery art has tried to please the child by placing before him the things an adult likes, in a form that would be understood by the child and be acceptable to him. It has been an attempt to share with the child an experience of something pleasurable and, by the act of sharing, to affirm the concept of 'us' rather than 'you'.

Nursery art has developed in the same way that the nursery has developed: from a tool of the parent to an aspect of the child's individuality, without losing sight of the fact that it is a family art. It reflects a change in attitude towards the child, from the concept of the infant as a fragile and precious doll enveloped in organdie and tulle for a daily ceremony of unpackaging and display, to one that treats him as a sentient being to be provided with surroundings that reflect his personality. Society nowadays is dedicated to the promotion of happiness in the child, and to its nurture rather than its suppression by too great or too little love. The aim is neither to smother nor to neglect. The nursery arose out of the need for a place in which the infant could be protected and encouraged to flourish until it was ready to be transplanted into the outside world. This encouragement is the *raison d'etre* for art for the nursery.

Every item of art for the nursery that is brought into the home is a measure of the health of a family relationship. In spite of the strangeness of some of the forms it has taken; in spite of some of the blind alleys it has sought to explore; in spite of its frequent bad taste and misapplication, it is the one feature that united the art of the Kate Greenaway baby, the Ida Rentoul Outhwaite fairy and the Disney Mickey Mouse. Nursery art rarely has any cosmic significance. It is not one of the more sublime manifestations of artistic endeavour, but its very existence, as evidence of man's capacity for love and the promotion of happiness in the youngest members of the family, shows it to be one of the higher attributes of the human spirit. An art which can arouse such feelings is rare. When it comes, it must be welcomed and encouraged.

Index